Insight And Responsibility

DATE DUE

BY ERIK H. ERIKSON

A Way of Looking at Things (Schlein, ed., 1987)
Childhood and Society (1950, 1963, 1985)
Young Man Luther (1958)
Insight and Responsibility (1964)
Identity: Youth and Crisis (1968)
Gandhi's Truth (1969)
Dimensions of a New Identity (1974)
Life History and the Historical Moment (1975)
Toys and Reasons (1977)
Identity and the Life Cycle (1959, 1980)
The Life Cycle Completed (1982)

EDITED BY ERIK H. ERIKSON
Adulthood (1978)

ERIK H. ERIKSON

Insight

AND

Responsibility

*Lectures on the Ethical Implications
of Psychoanalytic Insight*

W · W · NORTON & COMPANY

New York · London

Library of Congress Catalog Card No. 64-11136

ALL RIGHTS RESERVED

Published simultaneously in Canada by Stoddart,
a subsidiary of General Publishing Co. Ltd,
Don Mills, Ontario.

ISBN 0-393-09451-0

W. W. Norton & Company, Inc., 500 Fifth Avenue, New York, N.Y. 10110
PRINTED IN THE UNITED STATES OF AMERICA

1 2 3 4 5 6 7 8 9 0

Contents

Preface

It is not unusual to publish a series of lectures addressed to one and the same audience. The lectures published here, however, were given on three continents. Their unity, one might think, could lie only in the speaker's desire to repeat himself in widely distant places. Yet, while each lecture marked a different and distinct occasion, all but one of these occasions called for an *address*, and all converged on a common theme. A commemoration of Freud's hundredth birthday in Germany; a memorial lecture for a young psychiatrist; an "academic lecture" in my professional association; an address in India—on all of these occasions I felt called upon to speak of the light thrown by clinical insight on the responsibilities which each generation of men has for all succeeding ones. That the most common response among such a variety of listeners was the remark, "I look forward to reading it," may not necessarily signify the unmixed success of the spoken word, but it does add a reason for offering these lectures in print.

In revising them, I have endeavored to link the common

themes more clearly. I have also enlarged some lectures considerably, two to twice their size. The questions asked by a critical audience are often already answered in the lecturer's notes, that is, in just those passages which he chose to omit as relatively expendable. I have restored such passages here. On occasion, however, I have simply welcomed the opportunity of spelling out what I would have said had I not been restricted by requirements of time.

The level of discourse in these lectures is called insight. This is a form of discernment hard to define and harder to defend, for it includes those preconscious assumptions which both precede and follow proven knowledge and formulated theory, and it includes enlightened common sense and informed partisanship. Without all of these, the clinician can neither heal nor teach; while he often comes face to face with his insights only in the act of interpreting, advising, or, indeed, lecturing. By then, however, he may find himself formulating conceptions which must again be verified in systematic observation. Thus responsibility always renews itself.

If finding expression for such insights is one of the speaking clinician's tasks, and the building of theory another, then this book, by its nature, goes to the limit of the first task and will be found wanting in the second.

The geographic and thematic range of the lectures makes it impossible to thank all the individuals who helped in their planning and delivery, although I think of each occasion as a rare experience of challenge and friendship. The sponsoring organizations are noted at the beginning of each lecture. All but the last of the lectures were planned while I was on the staff of the Austen Riggs Center in Stockbridge and in the lifetime of my friend and critic David Rapaport. During the whole period I was partially or wholly supported by grants of the Ford Foundation and of the Shelter Rock Foundation to the Austen Riggs Center. The lectures were collected and revised during my fellowship in the Center for Advanced

Studies in the Behavorial Sciences during the spring of 1963.

Joan Erikson edited this book and has been, throughout, companion to its insights.

References are for the most part restricted to the acknowledgment of quotations. This leaves a number of debts of appreciation and of refutation as yet unpaid.

E.H.E.

Cotuit, Massachusetts

Acknowledgments

THE LECTURES IN THIS VOLUME have been published in earlier versions in various books and periodicals:

THE FIRST PSYCHOANALYST appeared in the *Yale Review*, 46:40–62, 1956, and was reprinted in *Freud and the Twentieth Century*, edited by Benjamin Nelson, Gloucester: Peter Smith, 1958.

THE NATURE OF CLINICAL EVIDENCE was first published in *Daedalus*, 87:65–87, 1958, and reprinted in *Evidence and Inference*, edited by Daniel Lerner, Glencoe: The Free Press, 1959.

IDENTITY AND THE UPROOTEDNESS OF OUR TIME was published in *Uprooting and Resettlement*, Bulletin of the World Federation for Mental Health, 1959.

HUMAN STRENGTH AND THE CYCLE OF GENERATIONS first appeared in the form of a much briefer paper, "The Roots of Virtue," in *The Humanist Frame*, edited by Sir Julian Huxley, New York: Harper and Bros., 1961.

PSYCHOLOGICAL REALITY AND HISTORICAL ACTUALITY appeared in a briefer version titled "Reality and Actuality" in *The Journal of the American Psychoanalytic Association*, 10:451–473, 1962.

THE GOLDEN RULE IN THE LIGHT OF NEW INSIGHT in its first form was published as "The Golden Rule and the Cycle of Life" in the *Harvard Medical Alumni Bulletin*, Vol. 37, No. 2, 1963, and was reprinted in *The Study of Lives*, edited by R. W. White, New York: Appleton-Century-Crofts, 1963.

In each case the lectures were revised and expanded for publication in their present form.

Heaven does with us as we with torches do
Not light them for themselves. For if our virtues
Did not go forth of us, 'twere all alike
As if we had them not.

—"Measure for Measure"

I

The First
Psychoanalyst

The 100th birthday of Sigmund Freud presented an occasion to introduce a new generation of German students to an event in the history of European thought which had been all but obliterated by National Socialist teaching: the discovery of psychoanalysis. The following address was delivered at a ceremony held jointly by the universities of Frankfurt and Heidelberg, at the University of Frankfurt, on May 6, 1956.

IT IS A SOLEMN and yet always a deeply incongruous occasion when we select an anniversary to honor a man who in lonely years struggled through a unique experience and won a new kind of knowledge for mankind. To some of us, the field created by Sigmund Freud has become an absorbing profession, to some an inescapable intellectual challenge, to all the promise (or threat) of an altered image of man. But any sense of proprietary pride in the man to be honored this year should be sobered by the thought that we have no right to assume that we would have met his challenge with more courage than his contemporaries did in the days when his insights were new. It seems fitting to use his centenary to review some of the dimensions of lonely discovery.

It is not easy (unless it be all too easy) for a "Freudian" to speak of the man who *was* Freud, of a man who grew to be a myth before our eyes. I knew Freud when he was very old, and I was young. Employed as a tutor in a family friendly to him I had the opportunity of seeing him on quiet occasions, with children and with dogs, and at outings in the mountains. I do not know whether I would have noticed Freud in a crowd. His notable features were not spectacular: the finely domed forehead, the dark, unfathomable eyes, and certain small indomitable gestures—they all had become part of that inner containment which crowns the old age of good fighters.

I was an artist then, which can be a European euphemism for a young man with some talent, but nowhere to go. What probably impressed me most was the fact that this doctor of the mind, this expert of warped biography, had surrounded himself in his study with a small host of little statues: those distilled variations of the human form which were created by the anonymous artists of the archaic Mediterranean. Certainly, of Freud's field, of conflict and complaint and confession, there was no trace in their art. This respect for form, so surprising in a man who had unearthed mankind's daimonic inner world, was also obvious in his love for proud dogs and for gaily bright children. I vaguely felt that I had met a man of rare dimensions, rare contradictions.

When I became a psychoanalyst myself, this same old man —now remote from the scene of training and gathering—became for me what he is for the world: the writer of superb prose, the author of what seems like more than one lifetime's collected works: a master, so varied in his grandiose one-sidedness that the student can manage to understand only one period of his work at a time. Strangely enough, we students knew little of his beginnings, nothing of that mysterious self-analysis which he alluded to in his writings. We knew people whom Freud had introduced into psychoanalysis, but psychoanalysis itself had, to all appearances, sprung from his head like Athena from the head of Zeus.

The early Freud became better known to us only a very few years ago, through the accidental discovery of intimate letters written before the turn of the century. They permitted us to envisage Freud the beginner, the first, and for a decade, the only, psychoanalyst. To pay homage to him means, in the passage of time, to acknowledge a lasting bond and yet also to take leave of what is now history.

FOR ORIENTATION and comparison, let us consider the circumstances of another discovery of the nineteenth century, the discovery of a man who was also lonely and calumniated, and who was also eventually recognized as a changer of man's image: Charles Darwin. Darwin came upon his evolutionary laboratory, the Galapagos Islands, on a voyage which was not part of an intended professional design. In fact, he had failed in medicine, not for lack of talent, it would seem, but partially because of an intellectual selectivity which forbade him to learn passively—a self-protective selectivity of the kind for which old Bernard Shaw, in retrospect, patted himself on the back when he said, "My memory rejects and selects; and its selections are not academic. . . . I congratulate myself on this."

Once embarked on the *Beagle*, however, and on his way to his "laboratory," Darwin showed that dogged, that prejudiced persistence which is one condition for an original mind's becoming a creative one. He now fully developed his superior gift, namely, "noticing things which easily escape attention, and observing them carefully." His physical stamina was inexhaustible. His mind proved ready for the laboratory and the laboratory seemed to have waited for him. He could fully employ sweeping configurations of thought which had ripened in him: cutting across existing classifications which assumed a parallel, linear origin of all species from a common pool of creation, he saw everywhere transitions, transmutations, variations, signs of a dynamic struggle for adaptation. The law of natural selection began to "haunt him." And he perceived that man must come under the same law: "I see no possible means of drawing the line and saying, here you must stop."

Darwin, at the age of twenty-seven, went home with his facts and theory, and traveled no more. He gave the scientific world a few papers primarily on geological subjects; then he withdrew to the country, to work for twenty years on the *Origin of Species:* he *made* it a long and lonely discovery. He now became physically incapacitated by insomnia, nausea, and chills. His doctor-father could not diagnose his disease, but declared his son too delicate for a career out in the world. The son became a life-long invalid. If his hypersensitivity was a sign of hereditary degeneracy, as some doctors believe, then there never was a degenerate guided more wisely in the utilization of his degeneracy by an inner genius of economy. For, "I could . . . collect facts bearing on the origin of species . . . when I could do nothing else from illness." Not that Darwin did not realize what this restriction of his lifespace did to him: when, at the end, even Shakespeare seemed so "intolerably dull" as to nauseate him, he deplored the "curious and lamentable loss of the higher aesthetic tastes" and spoke of an "enfeeblement of the emotional part of our nature."

I do not wish to speculate here on the dynamics of a psychoneurosis in a man like Darwin. But I do know that a peculiar malaise can befall those who have seen too much, who, in ascertaining new facts in a spirit seemingly as innocent as that of a child building with blocks, begin to perceive the place of these facts in the moral climate of their day. "We physicists have known sin," Oppenheimer has said; but it does not take the use of scientific data for mankind's material destruction to make a scientist feel or behave as if he had sinned. It is enough to have persisted, with the naïveté of genius, in the dissolution of one of the prejudices on which the security and the familiarity of the contemporary image of man is built. But a creative man has no choice. He may come across his supreme task almost accidentally. But once the issue is joined, his task proves to be at the same time intimately related to his most personal conflicts, to his superior selective perception, and to the stubbornness of his one-way will: he must court sickness, failure, or insanity, in order to test the alternative whether the established world will crush him, or whether he will disestablish a sector of this world's outworn fundaments and make place for a new one.

Darwin only dealt with man's biological origins. His achievement, and his "sin," was a theory that made man part of evolved nature. In comparing Darwin's approach to nature with his approach to man, a recent biographer remarks half-jokingly, "In any case, no man afflicted with a weak stomach and insomnia has any business investigating his own kind."

As we now turn to Freud, the psychological explorer, I hope to make the reader wonder whether anybody *but* one at least temporarily afflicted with psychosomatic symptoms, one temporarily sick of his own kind, could or would investigate his own species—provided that he had the inclination, the courage, and the mental means of facing his own neurosis with creative persistence. A man, I will submit, could begin to study man's inner world only by appointing his own neurosis that angel with whom he must wrestle and whom he must not let go until his blessing, too, has been given.

WHAT WAS Freud's Galapagos, what species fluttered what kinds of wings before his searching eyes? As has often been pointed out derisively, his creative laboratory was the neurologist's office, the dominant species hysterical ladies—"Fräulein Anna O.," "Frau Emmy v. N.," "Katarina" (not a Fräulein, because she was a peasant).

Freud was thirty when, in 1886, he became the private doctor of such patients. He had not expected to be a practitioner; he had, in fact, received his medical degree belatedly. His mind, too, had been "selective." At the age of seventeen he had chosen medicine, in preference to law and politics, when he heard Goethe's "Ode to Nature": the unveiling of nature's mysteries, not the healing of the sick, provided the first self-image of a doctor. Then came *his* professional moratorium. As in an ascetic reaction to romantic indulgence he committed himself to the physiological laboratory and to the monastic service of physicalistic physiology. What geology was to Darwin, physiology was to Freud: a schooling in method. The ideology of the physicalistic physiologic method of the time was formulated in an oath by two of its outstanding teachers, DuBois Reymond and Brücke: "to put in power this truth: No other forces than the common physical chemical ones are active within the organism. . . . One has either to find the specific way or form of their action by means of the physical mathematical method, or to assume new forces equal in dignity to the chemical physical forces inherent in matter." [1] *New forces equal in dignity*—we shall return to this phrase.

When Freud exchanged the academic monastery for the medical parsonage, he had fully developed a style of work which would have sufficed for an impressively productive lifetime. He had published many papers on physiological and neurological subjects, and had two major works in preparation. Thus, when he became a practicing neurologist, he left a future behind him. But he had married the girl who had waited for him, and he wanted a family, in fact, a large one; he had earned the right to have confidence in himself.

Yet, a future anticipated in a man's configurations of thought means more than time not yet spent. To give up the laboratory meant to relinquish a work-discipline and a work-ideology to which Freud had been deeply committed. The work of a specialist catering to the epidemiological market was lacking in what Freud nostalgically called an inner tyrant, i.e., a great principle. Luckily, he had met an older practitioner, Dr. Joseph Breuer, who had shown him that there was a laboratory hidden in the very practice of neurology.

Freud's new laboratory, then, were patients, mostly women, who brought him symptoms which only an overly-serious and searching observer could accept as constituting a field activated by dignified forces. These ladies suffered from neuralgic pains and anesthesias, from partial paralyses and contractions, from tics and convulsions, from nausea and finickiness, from the inability to see and from visual hallucinations, from the inability to remember and from painful floods of memory. Popular opinion judged the ladies to be spoiled, just putting on airs—"attention-getting" some of us would call it today. The dominant neuropathology of the day, however, assumed some of their disturbances to be a consequence of hereditary degenerative processes in the brain. Freud, too, had learned to treat these patients like partially decerebrated bundles, or like children without a will: he had learned to apply massage and electricity to the affected body part and to dominate the patient's will by hypnosis and suggestion. He might, for example, order the hypnotized patient to laugh out loud when encountering in the future a certain thought or a person or place, the sight of which had previously caused a fit or a paralysis. The awakened patient did laugh out loud, but more often than not, she would become afflicted again, and in connection with something else.

But Freud, like Darwin, could not believe in linear descent —in this instance, of isolated symptoms from defects of the brain. In an array of symptoms he, too, looked for a common principle, a struggle for equilibrium, a clash of forces. And he was convinced that challenging phenomena must have a hidden history. As Freud listened to his hypnotized patients, he realized that they were urgently, desperately offering him series of memories which, seemingly fragmentary, were like variations in search of a theme—a theme which was often found in a historical model event.

Here no detail could be too trivial for investigation. A patient suffers from a persistent illusion of smelling burned pancakes. All right, the smell of burned pancakes shall be the subject of exhaustive analysis. As this smell is traced to a certain scene and the scene vividly remembered, the sensation disappears, to be replaced by the smell of cigars. The smell of cigars is traced to other scenes, in which a man in an authoritative position was present, and in which disturbing subjects had been mentioned in a connection which demanded that the patient control her feelings.

It fits our image of those Victorian days—a time when children in all, and women in most circumstances were to be seen but not heard—that the majority of symptoms would prove to lead back to events when violently aroused affects (love, sex, rage, fear) had come into conflict with narrow standards of propriety and breeding. The symptoms, then, were delayed involuntary communications: using the whole body as spokesman, they were saying what common language permits common people to say directly: "He makes me sick," "She pierced me with her eyes," "I could not swallow that insult," or, as the song has it, "I'm gonna wash that man right out of my hair." Freud the neurologist now became "haunted" by the basic conviction that any neurotic symptom, traced along a path of associated experiences (not of neurological pathways), would lead to the revival in memory of earlier and earlier conflicts, and in doing so would yield a complete history of its origin.

As Freud proceeded with his reconstruction of the pasts of his patients, a dangerous insight dawned on him; such conflicts as his patients revealed were, in principle, shared by all men. It would be hard, indeed, "to draw the line and say here you must stop." He became aware of the fact that man, in principle, does not remember or understand much of what is most significant in his childhood, and more, that he does not want to. Here, a mysterious *individual prehistory* seemed to loom up, as important for psychology as Darwin's biological prehistory was for biology.

But Darwin had at his disposal the whole tradition of an ancient science. For Freud's psychologic findings, there were, at first, only physiologic methods, his own speculations, and the sayings of writers and philosophers, who, in their way, it seemed, had known it all. Yet, it appears to be part of a creative man's beginnings that he may change his field and yet maintain the manner of work which became part of his first identity as a worker. Freud had investigated the nature of brain lesions by slicing the brains of young animals and foeti. He now investigated memories as representative cross sections of a patient's emotional condition. In successive memories, he traced trends which led, like pathways, to the traumatic past; there experiences of a disruptive nature loomed like lesions interfering with growth. Thus, the search for traumatic events in the individual's forgotten prehistory, his early childhood, replaced the search for lesions in early development.

Psychology, of course, is the preferred field for a transfer of configurations of thought from other fields. The nature of things, or better, man's logical approach to things, is such that analogies—up to a point—reveal true correspondences. But the history of psychology also reveals how consistently neglectful and belated man is in applying to his own nature methods of observation which he has tried out on the rest of nature. That man, the observer, is in some essential way set off from the observed world, is clear. But this difference calls for a constant redefinition in the light of new modes of thought. Only thus can man keep wisely different rather than vainly so. Before Copernicus, vanity as well as knowledge insisted that the earth must be in the exact nodal center of God's universe. Well, we know now where we are. Before Darwin, man could claim a different origin from the rest of the animal world with whom he shares a slim margin of the earth's crust and atmosphere. Before Freud, man (that is, man of the male sex and of the better classes) was convinced that he was fully conscious of all there was to him, and sure of his divine values. Childhood was a mere training ground, in charge of that intermediary race, women.

In such a world female hysteria was implicitly acknowledged by men and men doctors as a symptom of the natural inferiority, the easy degeneracy, of women. When Freud presented to the Vienna Medical Society a case of *male* hysteria, the reaction of his colleagues convinced him that years of isolation lay ahead of him. He accepted it then and there: he never visited that society again. Yet, their reaction proved to be only one small aspect of a memorable crisis in which a new science was almost stillborn, by no means only because of professional isolation, but also because of disturbances in the instrument of observation, the observer's mind. Freud's early writings and letters permit us to see a threefold crisis: a crisis in therapeutic technique; a crisis in the conceptualization of clinical experience; and a personal crisis. I shall try to indicate in what way all three crises were, in essence, one, and that they were the necessary dimensions of discovery in psychology.

FIRST, THEN, Freud's change in technique. The textbooks describe it as the replacement of the cathartic and the suggestive methods by the psychoanalytic one. In Freud's *Studies in Hysteria*,[2] however, a pervasive change in the doctor-patient relationship is clearly traced. Freud judged some of his patients to be outstanding in character and talents, rather than degenerate. He began to let himself be led by the sequence and the nature of their communications. With amused surprise he would admit that a hypnotized patient, in suggesting to him that he should stop interrupting her with his authoritative suggestions, had a point. She fortified her point by unearthing memories which he would not have suspected. He realized that in hypnosis the patients had at their disposal a depth of understanding and a freedom of affect which they did not marshal in normal life. This he had not imposed by suggestion: it was their judgment and their affect, and if they had it in hypnosis, it was part of them. Perhaps, if he treated them like whole people, they would learn to realize the wholeness which was theirs. He now offered them a conscious and direct partnership: he made the patient's healthy, if submerged, part his partner in understanding the unhealthy part. Thus was established one basic principle of psychoanalysis, namely, that *one can study the human mind only by engaging the fully motivated partnership of the observed individual, and by entering into a sincere contract with him.*

But a contract has two partners, at least. The changed image of the patient changed the self-image of the doctor. He realized that habit and convention had made him and his fellow physicians indulge in an autocratic pattern, with not much more circumspection or justification than the very paternal authorities who he now felt had made the patients sick in the first place. He began to divine the second principle of psychoanalysis, namely, that *you will not see in another what you have not learned to recognize in yourself.* The mental healer must divide himself as well as the patient into an observer and an observed.

The intellectual task faced here, namely psychoanalytic insight and communication, was a massive one. Today, it is difficult to appreciate the psychosocial task involved. Freud had to relinquish a most important ingredient of the doctor role of the times: the all-knowing father role, which was safely anchored in the whole contemporary cult of the paternal male as the master of every human endeavor except the nursery and the kitchen. This should not be misunderstood: Freud did not, overnight, become a different man. Indeed, there are many who will see nothing in the nature of renunciation of paternalism in him. But we are not speaking here of opinions and roles in the modern sense, of personalities subject to change like the body styles of automobiles which retain little logical relation to the inner motor of the thing, nor to the laws of the road. True roles are a matter of a certain ideologicesthetic unity, not of opinions and appearances. True change is a matter of worthwhile conflict, for it leads through the painful consciousness of one's position to a new conscience in that position. As Justice Holmes once said, the first step toward a truer faith is the recognition that *I*, at any rate, am *not* God. Furthermore, roles anchored in work-techniques are prepared in the intricacies of a man's life history. Whoever has suffered under and identified with a stern father must become a stern father himself, or else find an entirely different quality of moral strength, an equal measure of strength. Young Martin Luther's religious crisis is a transcendent example of the heights and the depths of this problem.

Freud, as we have seen, had sought a new inner tyrant in a work-ideology shared with esteemed minds. He had relinquished it. Now, he discarded the practicing neurologist's prevailing role of dominance and of license. This, then, is the first aspect of Freud's crisis: he had to create a new therapeutic role for which there was no ideological niche in the tradition of his profession. He had to create it—or fail.

THE SECOND PROBLEM which isolated Freud in those years was the course taken by his search for the "energy of equal dignity" which might be the quantity and the power in mental life; for the mental mechanisms which normally maintain such power in a state of constancy; and for those inner conditions which unleash its destructiveness. The power, as we saw, was first perceived as "affect," the disturbance in the machine, as a "damming up." A long treatise recently found with some of Freud's letters reveals the whole extent of Freud's conflict between the creative urge to say in psychological terms what only literature had known before him, and on the other hand, his desperate obedience to physiology. The treatise is called "A Psychology for Neurologists." [3] It was written in 1895, sent to his friend Fliess, and forgotten. Freud introduces it thus: "The intention of this project is to furnish us with a psychology which shall be a natural science: its aim, that is, is to represent psychical processes as quantitatively determined states of specifiable material particles and so to make them plain and void of contradictions." Freud proceeds to develop a model for the organization of these "particles," a sensitive machine for the management of qualities and quantities of excitation, such as are aroused by external and internal stimuli. Physical concepts are combined with histological concepts to create a kind of neuronic Golem, a robot, in which even consciousness and thought are mechanistically explainable on the basis of an over-all principle of inner constancy. Here Freud, at the very beginning of his career as a psychologist, tried to create a mind-robot, a thinking-machine, in many ways related to the mechanical and economic as well as the physiological configurations of his day. As Freud wrote triumphantly to his friend: "Everything fell into place, the cogs meshed, the thing really seemed to be a machine which in a moment would run of itself." But one month after Freud had sent this conception to his friend, he recanted it. "All I was trying to do," he writes, "was to explain defense (against affect), but I found myself explaining something from the very heart of nature. I found myself wrestling with the whole of psychology. Now I want to hear no more of it." He now calls the psychology a "kind of aberration." This manuscript, found only accidentally, documents in a dramatic way the pains to which a discoverer will go *not* to haphazardly ignore the paths of his tradition, but to follow them instead to their absurd limit, and to abandon them only when the crossroad of lone search is reached.

In the meantime, clinical work had brought Freud within sight of his crossroad. His patients, he had become convinced, were suffering primarily from the "damming up" of one irrepressible "affect," namely, sexual sensuality, the existence of which had been consistently denied by their overclothed parents, while engaged in only with furtive shame and degradation by many of their mothers. In the epidemiological fact of widespread female hysteria, Freud faced the specific symptoms of the Victorian age, the price paid, especially by women, for the hypocritical double standard of the sexes in the dominant classes, the masters of commerce and the would-be masters of industrial power. However, the most glaring epidemiological fact (compare poliomyelitis, or juvenile delinquency) does not receive clarification until a seasoned set of theoretical configurations happens to suggest a specific approach. In introducing the energy concept of a sexual libido, which from birth onward is the fuel in all desiring and loving, and which our mind-machine must learn to transform according to our goals and ideals—in this concept Freud found at once the most fitting answer to the questions posed by his patients' memories, and the theory most consistent with his search for a "dignified force." But alas, it was also the most irrationally repugnant solution thinkable in his prudish times, and a solution of emotional danger to the observer. For, indeed, where "to draw the line"?

Here Freud's genetic fervor led to a faulty reconstruction. Certain of being on the right track, and yet shaken by inner and outer resistances, he overshot the mark. In search for a pathogenic Ur-event, he was led to regard as historically real the patients' accounts of passive sexual experiences in the first years of childhood, and to consider the fathers of the patients the perpetrators in such events. He later confessed: "The analysis had led by the correct path to such infantile sexual traumas, and yet, these were not true. Thus, the basis of reality had been lost. At that time, I would gladly have dropped the whole thing." But finally, "I reflected that if hysterics trace back their symptoms to imaginary traumas, then this new fact signified that they create such scenes in fantasy, and hence psychic reality deserves to be given a place next to actual reality." Freud would soon be able to describe psychic reality systematically as the domain of fantasy, dream, and mythology, and as the imagery and language of a universal unconscious, thus transforming into a scientific dimension what had been age-old intuitive knowledge.

In the meantime, had his error detracted from the "dignity" of sexuality? It does not seem so. Knowing what we know today, it is obvious that somebody had to come sometime who would decide that it would be better for the sake of the study of human motivation to call too many rather than too few things sexual, and then to modify the hypothesis by careful inquiry. For it was only too easy to do what had become civilization's "second nature," that is, in the face of the man's sexual and aggressive drives forever to beat a hasty retreat into romanticism and religionism, into secrecy, ridicule and lechery. The patients' fantasies were sexual, and something sexual must have existed in their early years. Freud later called that something *psychosexuality*, for it encompasses the fantasies as well as the impulses, the psychology as well as the biology in the earliest stages of human sexuality.

Today one can add that Freud's error was not even as great as it seemed. First of all, sexual (if not always genital) seductions of children do occur, and are dangerous to them. But more important, the general provocation and exploitation of the child's immature emotions by parent and grandparent for the sake of their own petty emotional relief, of suppressed vengefulness, of sensual self-indulgence, and of sly righteousness must be recognized not only as evident in case histories, but as a universal potentiality often practiced and hypocritically rationalized by very "moral" individuals, indeed. Samuel Butler's *The Way of All Flesh* is probably the most forceful statement on record. What today is decried as "momism" in the United States existed in analogous form in the father's role in the Victorian world: it is only necessary to think of Hitler's official account of his father-hate, and the appeal of this account for millions of young Germans, to know that this is a smoldering theme of general explosiveness. In finding access to the altogether fateful domain of man's prolonged childhood, Freud discovered that infantile man, in addition to and often under the guise of being trained, is being ruefully exploited, only to become in adulthood nature's most systematic and sadistic exploiter. Freud's search thus added another perspective of as yet unforeseeable importance to the image of man.

Yet, this discovery, too, had to pass through its lonely stage. Freud had made a significant mistake, and he was not one to shirk the responsibility for it either publicly or privately. He made it part of his self-analysis.

WE KNOW about this first self-analysis in history from the letters, already mentioned, which Freud wrote to Dr. Wilhelm Fliess of Berlin. The extent and the importance of Freud's friendship with Fliess was not even suspected until the letters revealed it.

The two doctors met for what they called their "congresses," long weekends in some mountainous city or town. Their common heritage of education permitted them to roam in varied conversation, as they walked vigorously through the countryside. Freud seems to have shared Nietzsche's impression that a thought not born in locomotion could not be much good. But among the theories discussed by the two doctors, there were many which never saw the light of publication. Thus, Fliess, for many years, was the first and only one to share Freud's thinking.

Psychoanalysts do not seem to like this friendship much; Fliess, after all, was not even a psychoanalyst. Some of us now read of Freud's affection for this man wishing we could emulate that biographer of Goethe who, in the face of Goethe's claim that at a certain time he had dearly loved a certain lady, remarks in a footnote: "Here Goethe is mistaken." Freud, we now say, must have overestimated this friendship in an irrational, almost pathological way. But what, after all, do thinkers need friends for? So that they can share speculations, each alternately playing benevolent authority to the other, each being the other's co-conspirator, each serving as applauding audience, and as cautioning chorus. Freud calls Fliess his "*Other* one," to whom he can entrust what is not ready for "the *others*." Fliess, at any rate, seems to have had the stature and the wide education which permitted Freud to entrust him with "imaginings, transpositions, and guesses." That Freud's imaginings turned out to be elements of a true vision and a blueprint for a science, while Fliess's ended in a kind of mathematical mysticism, provides no grounds to belittle the friendship. The value of a friend may sometimes be measured by the magnitude of the problem which we leave behind with him.

The friendship seems to have been unmarred by irrational disturbances, until, in 1894, Freud consulted Fliess in regard to his own symptoms and moods, which he condenses in the word *Herzelend*—something like "misery of the heart." Fliess had cauterized swellings in Freud's nose and had urged him to give up his beloved cigars. Suddenly, the intellectual communication appears jammed: "I have not looked at your excellent case histories," Freud writes, and indicates that his latest communication to Fliess "was abandoned in the middle of a sentence." He continues: "I am suspicious of you this time, because this heart business [*Herzangelegenheit*] of mine is the first occasion on which I have ever heard you contradict yourself." At this time, Freud speaks of his discoveries with the anguish of one who has seen a promised land which he must not set his foot on: "I have the distinct feeling," he writes, "that I have touched on one of the great secrets of nature." This tedium of thought seems to have joined the "heart misery" and was now joined by a mistrust of his friend. He wrote, "Something from the deepest depths of my own neurosis has ranged itself against my taking a further step in understanding of the neuroses, and you have somehow been involved."

Freud, at this point, had developed toward Fliess what later, when he understood it, he called a transference, i.e., that peculiar mixture of overestimation and mistrust, which man is so especially ready to bestow on people in significant positions—doctors and priests, leaders and kings, and other superiors, competitors, and adversaries. It is called transference, because, where it is neurotic, it is characterized by the blurring of an adult relationship through the transfer to it of infantile loves and hates, dependencies and impotent rages. Transference thus also implies a partial regression to childish attitudes. It was this very area which, at that time, Freud was trying to understand in his patients. Yet, in Freud, it was quite obviously related to the processes of creativity. We have seen how young Freud, in his student days, had subdued an almost incestuous eagerness to "unveil nature" by the compensatory concentration on laboratory work. He had thus postponed a conflict by realizing only one part of his identity. But when, in his words, he "touched on one of the secrets of nature," he was forced to realize that other, that more creative identity. For any refuge in the established disciplines of scientific inquiry was, as the project proved, forever closed. It is in those moments when our divided selves threaten to drag each other down, that a friend, as Nietzsche said, becomes the life-saver which keeps us afloat and together.

Freud thus discovered another principle in his new work, namely, that *psychological discovery is accompanied by some irrational involvement of the observer, and that it cannot be communicated to another without a certain irrational involvement of both*. Such is the stuff of psychology; here it is not enough to put on an armor of superiority or aloofness in the hope that, like the physicist's apron, it will protect vital organs against the radiation emanating from the observed. Here, only the observer's improved insight into himself can right the instrument, protect the observer, and permit the communication of the observed.

In his transference to Fliess, Freud recognized one of the most important transferences of all: the transfer of an early father-image on later individuals and events. And here we can recognize the pervasiveness in these crises of the great father theme. We saw this theme in Freud's determination not to play autocratic father to patients already crushed by autocracy; we recognized this theme as the core of his tendentious error in the genetic reconstruction of his patients' childhood; and we observe it in his filial reactions to Fliess. A dream, he now reported to Fliess, had clearly revealed to him the fact, and the explanation for the fact, that an irrational wish to blame all fathers for their children's neuroses had dominated him. Yet, one senses at the same time the need of the creative man to have his creativity sired, as it were, by an overvalued friend —a need which often leads, and in Freud's life periodically led, to almost tragicomic involvements.

Having established, then, both the actual and the fantastic aspects of a universal father-image, Freud now could break through to the first prehistoric *Other* of them all: the loving mother. He was free to discover the whole Oedipus complex, and to recognize it as a dominant theme in literature and in mythologies around the world. Only then could he understand the full extent to which he, when sick and bewildered, had made a parent-figure out of Fliess, so that that mystic *Other* might help him analyze himself "as if he were a stranger." He concluded that "self-analysis is really impossible, otherwise there would be no illness . . . I can only analyze myself with objectively acquired knowledge." This insight is the basis for what later became the training analysis, that is, the preventive and didactic psychoanalytic treatment of every prospective psychoanalyst.

The friendship, for other reasons too, had outlived itself. It ended when Freud, in a way, could least afford to lose it, namely, around the turn of the century, after the appearance of *The Interpretation of Dreams*.[4] Freud then, as later, considered this book his most fundamental contribution; he then also believed it to be his last. And, as he wrote, "not a leaf has stirred." For months, for years, there were no book reviews, no sales to speak of. Where there was interest, it was mostly disbelief and calumniation. At this time, Freud seems temporarily to have despaired of his medical way of life. Fliess offered a meeting at Easter. But this time Freud refused. "It is more probable that I shall avoid you," he writes. "I have conquered my depression, and now . . . it is slowly healing. . . . In your company . . . your fine and positive biological discoveries would rouse my innermost (impersonal) envy. . . . I should unburden my woes to you and come back dissatisfied . . . no one can help me in what depresses me, it is my cross, which I must bear." A few letters later, he refers to his patients' tendency to prolong the treatment beyond the acquisition of the necessary insight: "Such prolongation is a compromise between illness and health which patients themselves desire, and . . . the physician must therefore not lend himself to it." It is clear that he has now recognized such "prolongation" and "compromise" in his friendship as well, and that he will refuse to permit himself a further indulgence in the dependence on Fliess. But he will sorely miss him—"my one audience," as he calls him.

In the course of this friendship a balance was righted: feminine intuition, childlike curiosity, and artistic freedom of style were recognized and restored as partners of the masculine "inner tyrant" in the process of psychological discovery. And Fliess? According to him the friendship was ship-wrecked on the age-old rock of disputed priorities: Freud, he said, envied him. And, indeed, Freud had expressed envy that Fliess worked "with light, not darkness, with the sun and not the unconscious." But it does not seem probable that Freud would have changed places with him.

THESE, THEN, were the dimensions of the crisis during which and through which psychoanalysis was born. During these years Freud at times expressed some despair and confessed to some neurotic symptoms which reveal phenomenological aspects of a creative crisis. He suffered from a "railroad phobia" and from acute fears of an early death—both symptoms of an over-concern with the all too rapid passage of time. "Railroad phobia" is an awkwardly clinical way of translating what in German is *Reisefieber*—a feverish combination of pleasant excitement and anxiety. But it all meant, it seems, on more than one level that he was "coming too late," that he was "missing the train," that he would perish before reaching some "promised land." He could not see how he could complete what he had visualized if every single step took so much "work, time and error." As is often the case, such preoccupation with time leads to apprehension centered in the heart, that metronome and measure of endurance.

In the letters the theme of time overlaps with a geographic restlessness. He thinks of emigrating, maybe to Berlin, to England, or to America. Most striking is a theme of European dimensions, namely, an intense, a "deeply neurotic" urge to see Rome. At first, he wants to arrange to meet his friend, his "one audience," there. But he writes, "We are not in Rome yet," or, "I am further away from Rome than at any time since we met, and the freshness of youth is notably declining." Only when his fundamental work, *The Interpretation of Dreams* is published, does Freud decide to spend Easter in Rome: "Not that there is any justification for it, I have achieved nothing yet [*es is nichts erreicht*] and in any case, circumstances will probably make it impossible."

What did Rome mean to Freud? It was a highly "overdetermined" and thus a highly condensed theme. We recognize in it the fate of Hannibal, who had kindled the imagination of the Jewish boy: the Semitic warlord had never conquered Rome. Beyond this, the Eternal City is the goal of many roads, all of which are superbly condensed in the final wish which Freud sent to Fliess: "Next Easter in Rome." Here we recognize the educated German's eternal *Sehnsucht* for Italy ("*dahin, dahin*"); the Israelite's longing for the ancestral home as expressed in the prayer at Passover, "Next year in Jerusalem"; and within it all a remnant of that infantile wonder once experienced by the little Jewish boy on the holiday of resurrection, under the eager guidance of the Kinderfrau, his Catholic nanny. I know that this kind of "over-determination," embracing various periods of a man's life and, at the same time, reconciling ambivalent divisions in his affects and in his imagery, seems to lack the parsimony of other sciences: but such is the material of psychoanalysis.

Only in the very last of the letters to Fliess does Freud seem to have found his position in time and space: "I have readers . . . the time is not yet ripe for followers." The last letter, written in the last year of the 19th century, admits, "We are terribly far ahead of our time." Freud is now forty-four years of age.

But lest anyone form the faulty image of a lamentably torn and tormented man and physician, it must be reported that the Freud of those years was what to all appearances we would call a well-adjusted individual, and what then was a decent and able one: a man who took conscientious care of all the patients who found their way to his door, who with devotion and joy raised a family of six children, who was widely-read and well-groomed, traveled with curiosity, walked (or, as we would say, exercised) with abandon, loved good food and wine wisely, and his cigars unwisely. His "railroad phobia" did not keep him from traveling. And, when he wrote about his being "arbeitsunfaehig" (unable to work), he meant that his writing was not keeping up with his aspirations. But he was not too "well-adjusted" to entertain the dreams, the passions, and the fears adhering to extraordinary vision; nor too "decent" to approach a few things in life with decisive, with ruthless integrity. All of which in a way he could ill afford, for the times were bad for a medical specialist; it was the time of one of the first economic depressions of the modern industrial era, it was a time of poverty in plenty. Nor did the self-analysis "reform" or chasten Freud. Some of the vital conflicts which pervaded the friendship with Fliess remained lifelong, as did some of the early methodological habits: in *Totem and Taboo*, Freud again reconstructed—this time on the stage of history—an "event" which, though an unlikely happening in past actuality, yet proved most significant as a timeless theme. But that early period of Freud's work gave to the new method of inquiry its unique direction, and with it gave its originator that peculiar unity of peculiarities which makes up a man's identity, thus forming the cornerstone of his kind of integrity, and posing his challenge to contemporaries and generations to come.

Freud's self-revelations in the *Interpretation of Dreams* as well as in his letters have provided ample leeway to both his friends and his adversaries for placing emphasis on one or the other of the inner contradictions which characterize genius. Any exclusive emphasis, however, on the infantile or the great, the neurotic or the creative, the emotional or the intellectual, the medical or the psychological aspects of a creative crisis sacrifices essential components. Here, I like to quote a sentence which Professor Cornford puts into the mouth of Pythagoras: "What is your warrant for valuing one part of my experience and rejecting the rest? If I had done so, you would never have heard my name."

THE UNIQUE DIRECTION given by Freud to the new method of inquiry consisted of the introduction into psychology of a system of co-ordinates which I can only summarize most briefly. His early energy concept provided the *dynamic-economic* co-ordinate, dealing with drives and forces and their transformations. A *topographic-structural* co-ordinate emerged from his study of the partitions within that early mind-robot; while the *genetic* co-ordinate takes account of the origin and the development in stages of both drive and structure.[5] Generations of psychoanalysts have endeavored to find proper places for each new observation and each new theory in these co-ordinates, which thus have provided a method of cross-checking not easily appreciated by the untrained. On the other hand, Freud's case-studies have given to the study of lives a daimonic depth to be found before him only in drama, in fiction, and in the confessions of men endowed with passionate introspection.

Since those early days of discovery, psychoanalysis has established deep and wide interrelationships with other methods of investigation, with methods of naturalist observation, of somatic examination, of psychological experiment, of anthropological field work, and of historical research. If, instead of enlarging on all these, I have focused on the early days, and on the uniqueness of the original Freudian experience, I have done so because I believe that an innovator's achievement can be seen most dramatically in that moment when he, alone against historical adversity and inner doubts, and armed only with the means of persuasion, gives a new direction to human awareness—new in its focus, new in its method, and new in its inescapable responsibility.

The dimensions of Freud's discovery are contained in a triad which, in a variety of ways, remains basic to the practice of psychoanalysis, but also to its application. It is the triad of a *therapeutic contract*, a *conceptual design*, and *systematic self-analysis*.

In psychoanalytic practice, this triad can never become routine. As new categories of suffering people prove amenable to psychoanalytic therapy, new techniques come to life, new aspects of the mind find clarification, and new therapeutic roles are created. Today, the student of psychoanalysis receives a training psychoanalysis which prepares him for the emotional hazards of his work. But he must live with the rest of mankind in this era of what we may call anxiety-in-plenty, and neither his personal life nor the very progress of his work will spare him renewed conflicts, be his profession ever so recognized, ever so organized. Wide recognition and vast organization, in fact, will not assure—they may even endanger—the basic triad, for which the psychoanalyst makes himself responsible, to wit: that as a clinician he accept his contract with the patient as the essence of his field of study and relinquish the security of seemingly more "objective" methods; that as a theorist he maintain a sense of obligation toward continuous conceptual redefinition and resist the lure of seemingly more profound or of more pleasing philosophic short cuts; and finally, that as a humanist he put self-observant vigilance above the satisfaction of seeming professional omnipotence. The responsibility is great. For, in a sense, the psychoanalytic method must remain forever a "controversial" tool, a tool for the detection of that aspect of the total image of man which in a given historical period is being neglected or exploited, repressed or suppressed by the prevailing technology and ideology—including hasty "psychoanalytic" ideologies.

Freud's triad remains equally relevant in the applications of psychoanalysis to the behavioral sciences, and to the humanities. An adult studying a child, an anthropologist studying a tribe, or a sociologist studying a riot sooner or later will be confronted with data of decisive importance for the welfare of those whom he is studying, while the strings of his own motivation will be touched, sometimes above and sometimes well below the threshold of awareness. He will not be able, for long, to escape the necessary conflict between his emotional participation in the observed events and the methodological rigor required to advance his field and human welfare. Thus, his studies will demand, in the long run, that he develop the ability to include in his observational field his human obligations, his methodological responsibilities, and his own motivations. In doing so, he will, in his own way, repeat that step in scientific conscience which Freud dared to make.

THAT SHIFT IN SELF-AWARENESS, however, cannot remain confined to professional partnerships such as the observer's with the observed, or the doctor's with his patient. It implies a fundamentally new *ethical orientation of adult man's relationship to childhood:* to his own childhood, now behind and within him; to his own child before him; and to every man's children around him.

But the fields dealing with man's historical dimension are far apart in their appraisal of childhood. Academic minds, whose long-range perspectives can ignore the everyday urgencies of the curative and educative arts, blithely go on writing whole world histories without a trace of women and children, whole anthropological accounts without any reference to the varying styles of childhood. As they record what causal chain can be discerned in political and economic realities, they seem to shrug off as historical accidents due to "human nature" such fears and rages in leaders and masses as are clearly the residue of childish emotions. True, scholars may have been justly repelled by the first enthusiastic intrusion of doctors of the mind into their ancient disciplines. But their refusal to consider the historical relevance of human childhood can be due only to that deeper and more universal emotional aversion and repression which Freud himself foresaw. On the other hand, it must be admitted that in clinical literature (and in literature turned altogether clinical) aversion has given place to a faddish preoccupation with the more sordid aspects of childhood as though they were the final determinants of human destiny.

Neither of these trends can hinder the emergence of a new

truth, namely that the collective life of mankind, in all its historical lawfulness, is fed by the energies and images of successive generations; and that each generation brings to human fate an inescapable conflict between its ethical and rational aims and its infantile fixations. This conflict helps drive man toward the astonishing things he does—and it can be his undoing. It is a condition of man's humanity—and the prime cause of his bottomless inhumanity. For whenever and wherever man abandons his ethical position, he does so only at the cost of massive regressions endangering the very safeguards of his nature.

Freud revealed this regressive trend by dissecting its pathological manifestations in individuals. But he also pointed to what is so largely and so regularly lost in the ambivalent gains of civilization: he spoke of "the child's radiant intelligence" —the naive zest, the natural courage, the unconditional faith of childhood which become submerged by excessive ambitions, by fearful teaching and by limited and limiting information.

Now and again, we are moved to say that a genius preserved in himself the clear eye of the child. But do we not all too easily justify man's mass regressions by pointing to the occasional appearance of leaders of genius? Yet, we know (and are morbidly eager to know) how tortured a genius can be by the very history of his ascendance, and how often a genius is driven to destroy with one hand as he creates with the other.

In Freud, a genius turned a new instrument of observation back on his childhood, back on all childhood. He invented a specific method for the detection of that which universally spoils the genius of the child in every human being. In teaching us to recognize the daimonic evil in children, he urged us not to smother the creatively good. Since then, the nature of growth in childhood has been studied by ingenious observers all over the world: never before has mankind known more about its own past—phylogenetic and ontogenetic. Thus, we may see Freud as a pioneer in a self-healing, balancing trend in human awareness. For now that technical invention readies itself to conquer the moon, generations to come may well be in need of being more enlightened in their drivenness, and more conscious of the laws of individuality; they may well need to appreciate and to preserve more genuine childlikeness in order to avoid utter cosmic childishness.

FREUD, BEFORE HE went into medicine, wanted to become a lawyer and politician, a lawmaker, a *Gesetzgeber*. When, in 1938, he was exiled from his country, he carried under his arm a manuscript on Moses, the supreme law-giver of the Jewish people whose unique fate and whose unique gifts Freud had accepted as his own. With grim pride he had chosen the role of one who opens perspectives on fertile fields to be cultivated by others. As we look back to the beginnings of his work, and forward to its implications, we may well venture to say: Freud the physician in finding a method of healing himself in the very practice of emotional cure has given a new, a psychological rationale for man's laws. He has made the decisive step toward a true interpenetration of the psychological with the technological and the political in the human order.

If, in the meantime, others see in him primarily the destroyer of precious illusions, if not of essential values, I would remind you of an event that took place in this city, Frankfurt am Main. It was from here that, in 1930, the Secretary of the Goethe Prize Committee informed Freud of his award, which was later received for her ailing father by Anna Freud, in a ceremony in the old (and now rebuilt) *Roemer*. In his dedication the Secretary suggested that "the Mephistophelic bend toward ruthless disillusion was the inseparable counterpart of the Faustian veneration of man's creative potentials." In his letter of acceptance Freud affirmed that nobody had recognized more clearly his "innermost personal motives."

II

The Nature of
Clinical Evidence

The first lecture focused on the origin (and the originator) of psychoanalysis at the turn of the century. The second is an exposition of the meaning of clinical experience for a psychoanalyst half a century later. This lecture was given as a contribution to an interdisciplinary symposium on "Evidence and Inference" at the Massachusetts Institute of Technology, in 1957.

THE LETTER which invited me to this symposium puts into the center of my assignment the question, *"How does a . . . clinician really work?"* It gives me generous latitude by inquiring about the psychotherapist's reliance on *intuition* ("or some other version of personal judgment") or on *objectified tests* ("relatively uniform among clinicians of different theoretical persuasions"). And it concludes: "To the extent that intuition plays a role, in what way does the clinician seek to discipline its operation: by his conceptual framework? by long personal experience?" This emphasizes, within the inquiry of how a clinician works, the question of how he thinks.

Such an invitation is a hospitable one, encouraging the guest, as it were, to come as he is. It spares the clinician whatever temptation he might otherwise feel to claim inclusion in the social register of long established sciences by demonstrating that he, too, can behave the way they do. He can state from the outset that all four: intuition and objective data, conceptual framework and experience are acceptable as the corners of the area to be staked out; but also, that in one lecture he can offer no more than phenomenological groundwork of a markedly personal nature.

The invitation in my case is addressed to a psychotherapist of a particular "persuasion": my training is that of Freudian psychoanalyst, and I help in the training of others—in the vast majority physicians—in this method. I shall place vocation over persuasion and try to formulate how the nature of clinical evidence is determined by a clinician's daily task. If I, nevertheless, seem to feel beholden to Freud's conceptual system— that is, a system originated around the turn of this century by a physician schooled in physicalist physiology—the reason is not narrowly partisan: few will deny that from such transfer of physicalistic concepts to psychology new modes of clinical thinking have developed in our time.

"Clinical," of course, is an old word. It can refer to the priest's administrations at the deathbed as well as to medical ministrations to the sick. In our time and in the Western world, the scope of the clinical is expanding rapidly to include not only medical but also social considerations, not only physical well-being but also mental health, not only matters of cure but also of prevention, not only therapy but also research. This means that clinical work is now allied with many brands of evidence and overlaps with many methodologies. In the Far East, the word "clinical" is again assuming an entirely different historical connotation, insofar as it concerns mind at all: in Communist China the "thought analyst" faces individuals considered to be in need of reform. He encourages sincere confessions and self-analyses in order to realign thoughts with "the people's will." There is much, infinitely much to learn about the ideological implications of concepts of mental sickness, of social deviancy, and of psychological cure. Yet, I feel called upon to speak of the nature of evidence gathered in the psychotherapeutic encounter.

Let me briefly review the elements making up the clinical

core of medical work as the encounter of two people, one in need of help, the other in the possession of professional methods. Their *contract* is a therapeutic one: in exchange for a fee, and for information revealed in confidence, the therapist promises to act for the benefit of the individual patient, within the ethos of the profession. There usually is a *complaint*, consisting of the description of more or less circumscribed pain or dysfunction, and there are *symptoms*, visible or otherwise localizable. There follows an attempt at an *anamnesis*, an etiological reconstruction of the disturbance, and an *examination*, carried out by means of the physician's naked senses or supported by instruments, which may include laboratory methods. In evaluating the evidence and in arriving at diagnostic and prognostic inferences (which are really the clinical form of a *prediction*), the physician *thinks clinically*—that is, he scans in his mind different *models* in which different modes of knowledge have found condensation: the *anatomical* structure of the body, the *physiological* functioning of body parts, or the *pathological* processes underlying classified disease entities. A clinical prediction takes its clues from the complaint, the symptoms, and the anamnesis, and makes inferences based on a rapid and mostly preconscious cross-checking against each other of anatomical, physiological and pathological models. On this basis, a *preferred method of treatment* is selected. This is the simplest clinical encounter. In it the patient lends parts of himself to an examination and as far as he possibly can, ceases to be a person, i.e., a creature who is more than the sum of its organs.

Any good doctor knows, however, that the patient's complaint is more extensive than his symptom, and the state of sickness more comprehensive than localized pain or dysfunction. As an old Jew put it (and old Jews have a way of speaking for the victims of all nations): "Doctor, my bowels are sluggish, my feet hurt, my heart jumps—and you know, Doctor, I myself don't feel so well either." The treatment is thus not limited to local adjustments; it must, and in the case of a "good" doctor automatically does, include a wider view of the complaint, and entail corresponding *interpretations* of the symptom to the patient, often making the "patient himself" an associate observer and assistant doctor. This is especially important, as subsequent appointments serve a *developing treatment-history*, which step by step verifies or contradicts whatever predictions had been made and put to test earlier.

This, then, for better or for worse, is the traditional core of the clinical encounter, whether it deals with physical or with mental complaints. But in the special case of the *psychotherapeutic encounter,* a specimen of which I intend to present and to analyze presently, three items crowd out all the others, namely, *complaint, anamnesis,* and *interpretation.* What goes on in the therapist's mind between the verbal complaint addressed to him and the verbal interpretation given in return—this, I take it, is the question to be examined here. But this means: in what way can the psychological clinician make his own perception and thought reliable in the face of the patient's purely verbal and social expression, and in the absence of nonverbal supportive instruments? At this point I am no longer quite so sure that the invitation to "tell us how a . . . clinician really works" was so entirely friendly, after all. For you must suspect that the psychotherapist, in many ways, uses the setting and the terminology of a medical and even a laboratory approach, claiming recourse to an anatomy, a physiology, and a pathology of the mind, without matching the traditional textbook clarity of medical science in any way. To put it briefly, the element of subjectivity, both in the patient's complaints and in the therapist's interpretations, may be vastly greater than in a strictly medical encounter, although this element is in principle not absent from any clinical approach.

Indeed, there is no choice but to put subjectivity in the center of an inquiry into evidence and inference in such clinical work as I am competent to discuss. The psychotherapist shares with any clinician the Hippocratic fact that hour by hour he must fulfill a *contract* with individuals who offer themselves to cure and study. They surrender much of their most personal inviolacy in the expectation that they will emerge from the encounter more whole and less fragmented than when they entered it. The psychotherapist shares with all clinicians the further requirement that even while facing most intimate and emotional matters, he must maintain intellectual inner contact with his conceptual models, however crude they may be. But more than any other clinician the psychotherapist must include in his field of observation a *specific self-awareness* in the very act of perceiving his patient's actions and reactions. I shall claim that there is a core of *disciplined subjectivity* in clinical work—and this both on the side of the therapist and of the patient—which it is neither desirable nor possible to replace altogether with seemingly more objective methods— methods which originate, as it were, in the machine-tooling of other kinds of work. How the two subjectivities join in the kind of disciplined understanding and shared insight which we think are operative in a cure—that is the question.

First, a word about "history taking," as the anamnesis is called today. In clinics, this is often done by "intake" workers, as if a patient, at the moment of entering treatment, could give an objective history of his sickness, and could reserve until later a certain fervent surrender to "the doctor." In the treatment proper, of course, much of this history will be reported again in significant moments. Whether or not the psychotherapist will then choose to dwell on the patient's past, however, he will enter his life history and join the grouping of individuals already significant in it. Therefore, without any wish to crowd him, I think I would feel methodologically closest to the historian in this symposium.

R. G. Collingwood defines as an historical process one "in

which the past, so far as it is historically known, survives
in the present." Thus being "itself a process of thought . . .
it exists only in so far as the minds which are parts of it know
themselves for parts of it." And again: "History is the life of
mind itself which is not mind except so far as it *both lives in
historical process and knows itself as so living*." [1]

However, it is not my task to argue the philosophy of history. The analogy between the clinician and the historian
as defined by Collingwood to me centers in the case-historian's
function in the art of history-taking, of becoming part of a
life history. Here the analogy breaks down; it could remain
relevant only if the historian were also a kind of clinical statesman, correcting events as he records them, and recording
changes as he directs them. Such a conscious clinician-historian-
statesman may well emerge in the future.

Let me restate the psychotherapeutic encounter, then, as an
historical one. A person has declared an emergency and has
surrendered his self-regulation to a treatment procedure. Besides having become a subjective *patient*, he has accepted the
role of a formal *client*. To some degree, he has had to interrupt his autonomous life-history as lived in the unself-conscious
balances of his private and his public life in order, for a while,
to "favor" a part-aspect of himself and to observe it with the
diagnostic help of a curative method. "Under observation," he
becomes self-observant. As a patient he is inclined, and as a
client often encouraged, to historicize his own position by
thinking back to the onset of the disturbance, and to ponder
what world order (magic, scientific, ethical) was violated and
must be restored before his self-regulation can be reassumed.
He participates in becoming a *case*, a fact which he may live
down socially, but which, nevertheless, may forever change
his view of himself.

The clinician, in turn, appointed to judge the bit of interrupted life put before him, and to introduce himself and his
method into it, finds himself part of another man's most inti-

mate life history. Luckily he also remains the functionary of a healing profession with a systematic orientation, based on a coherent world image—be it the theory that a sick man is beset by evil spirits or under the temptation of the devil, the victim of chemical poisons or of faulty heritage, racked by inner conflicts, or blinded by a dangerous ideology. In inviting his client to look at himself with the help of professional theories and techniques, the clinician makes himself part of the client's life history, even as the client becomes a case in the history of healing.

In northern California I knew an old Shaman woman who laughed merrily at my conception of mental disease, and then sincerely—to the point of ceremonial tears—told me of her way of sucking the "pains" out of her patients. She was as convinced of her ability to cure and to understand as I was of mine. While occupying extreme opposites in the history of American psychiatry, we felt like colleagues. This feeling was based on some joint sense of the historical relativity of all psychotherapy: the relativity of the patient's outlook on his symptoms, of the role he assumes by dint of being a patient, of the kind of help which he seeks, and of the kinds of help which are eagerly offered or are available. The old Shaman woman and I disagreed about the locus of emotional sickness, what it "was," and what specific methods would cure it. Yet, when she related the origin of a child's illness to the familial tensions existing within her tribe, when she attributed the "pain" (which had got "under a child's skin") to his grandmother's sorcery (ambivalence), I knew she dealt with the same forces, and with the same kinds of conviction, as I did in my professional nook. This experience has been repeated in discussions with colleagues who, although not necessarily more "primitive," are oriented toward different psychiatric persuasions.

The disciplined psychotherapist of today finds himself heir to medical methods and concepts, although he may decide to counteract these with a determined turn to existential or social

views concerning his person-to-person encounter in the therapeutic setting. At any rate, he recognizes his activities as a
function of life-historical processes, and concludes that in his
sphere one makes history as one records it.

IT IS IN SUCH apparent quicksand that we must follow the
tracks of clinical evidence. No wonder that often the only
clinical material which impresses some as being at all "scientific" is the more concrete evidence of the auxiliary methods
of psychotherapy—neurological examination, chemical analysis, sociological study, psychological experiment, etc.—all of
which, strictly speaking, put the patient into non-therapeutic
conditions of observation. Each of these methods may "objec-
tify" *some* matters immensely, provide inestimable supportive
evidence for *some* theories, and lead to independent methods
of cure in *some* classes of patients. But it is not of the nature
of the evidence provided in the psychotherapeutic encounter
itself.

To introduce such evidence, I need a specimen. This will
consist of my reporting to you what a patient *said* to me, how
he *behaved* in doing so and what I, in turn, *thought* and *did*—
a highly suspect method. And, indeed, we may well stand at
the beginning of a period when consultation rooms (already
airier and lighter than Freud's) will have, as it were, many
more doors open in the direction of an enlightened community's resources, even as they now have research windows in
the form of one-way screens, cameras, and recording equipment. For the kind of evidence to be highlighted here, however, it is still essential that, for longer periods or for shorter
ones, these doors be closed, soundproof, and impenetrable.

By emphasizing this I am not trying to ward off legitimate
study of the setting from which our examples come. I know
only too well that many of our interpretations seem to be of
the variety of that given by one Jew to another in a Polish

railroad station. "Where are you going?" asked the first. "To Minsk," said the other. "To Minsk!" exclaimed the first, "you say you go to Minsk so that I should believe you go to Pinsk! You are going to Minsk anyway—so why do you lie?" There is a widespread prejudice that the psychotherapist, point for point, uncovers what he claims the patient "really," and often unconsciously, had in mind, and that he has sufficient Pinsk-Minsk reversals in his technical arsenal to come out with the flat assertion that the evidence is on the side of his claim. It is for this very reason that I will try to demonstrate what method there may be in clinical judgment. I will select as my specimen the most subjective of all data, a dream-report.

A young man in his early twenties comes to his therapeutic hour about midway during his first year of treatment in a psychiatric hospital and reports that he has had the most disturbing dream of his life. The dream, he says, vividly recalls his state of panic at the time of the "mental breakdown" which had caused him to interrupt his studies for missionary work abroad and enter treatment. He cannot let go of the dream; it seemed painfully real on awakening; and even in the hour of reporting, the dream-state seems still vivid enough to threaten the patient's sense of reality. He is afraid that this is the end of his sanity.

THE DREAM: "There was a big face sitting in a buggy of the horse-and-buggy days. The face was completely empty, and there was horrible, slimy, snaky hair all around it. I am not sure it wasn't my mother." The dream report itself, given with wordy plaintiveness, is as usual followed by a variety of seemingly incidental reports of the events of the previous day which, however, eventually give way to a rather coherent account of the patient's relationship with his deceased grandfather, a country parson. In fact, he sees himself as a small boy with his grandfather crossing a bridge over a brook, his tiny hand in the old man's reassuring fist. Here the patient's mood changes to a deeply moved and moving admission of desperate nostalgia for the rural setting in which the values of his Nordic immigrant forebears were clear and strong.

How did the patient get from the dream to the grandfather? Here I should point out that we consider a patient's "associations" our best leads to the meaning of an as yet obscure item brought up in a clinical encounter, whether it is a strong affect, a stubborn memory, an intensive or recurring dream, or a transitory symptom. By associated evidence we mean everything which comes to the patient's mind during and after the report of that item. Except in cases of stark disorganization of thought, we can assume that what we call the synthesizing function of the ego will tend to associate what "belongs together," be the associated items ever so remote in history, separate in space, and contradictory in logical terms. Once the therapist has convinced himself of a certain combination in the patient of character, intelligence, and a wish to get well, he can rely on the patient's capacity to produce during a series of therapeutic encounters a sequence of themes, thoughts, and affects which seek their own concordance and provide their own cross-references. It is, of course, this basic synthesizing trend in clinical material itself which permits the clinician to observe with "free-floating attention," to refrain from undue interference, and to expect sooner or later a confluence of the patient's search for curative clarification and his own endeavor to recognize and to name what is most relevant, that is, to give an *interpretation*.

At the same time, everything said in an hour is linked with the material of previous appointments. It must be understood that whatever insight can result from one episode will owe its meaning to the fact that it clarifies previous questions and complements previous half-truths. Such *evidential continuity* can be only roughly sketched here; even to account for this one hour would take many hours. Let me only mention, then, the seemingly paradoxical fact that during his previous hour the patient had spoken of an increased well-being in his work and in his life, and had expressed trust in and even something akin to affection for me.

As to the rest of the hour of the dream-report I listened to the patient, who faced me in an easy chair, with only occasional interruptions for the clarification of facts or feelings. Only at the conclusion of the appointment did I give him a résumé of what sense his dream had made to me. It so happened that this interpretation proved convincing to us both and, in the long run, strategic for the whole treatment. (These are the hours we like to report.)

As I turn to the task of indicating what inferences helped me to formulate one of the most probable of the many possible meanings of this dream-report, I must ask you to join me in what Freud has called "free-floating attention," which—as I must now add—turns inward to the observer's ruminations even as it attends the patient's "free associations" and which, far from focusing on any one item too intentionally, rather waits to be impressed by recurring themes. These themes will, first faintly but ever more insistently, signal the nature of the patient's message and its meaning. It is, in fact, the gradual establishment of strategic intersections on a number of tangents that eventually makes it possible to locate in the observed phenomena that central core which comprises the "evidence."

I will now try to report what kinds of considerations will pass through a psychotherapist's mind, some fleetingly, others with persistent urgency, some hardly conscious in so many words, others nearly ready for verbalization and communication.

Our patient's behavior and report confront me with a therapeutic crisis, and it is my first task to perceive where the patient stands as a client, and what I must do next. What a clinician must do first and last depends, of course, on the setting of his work. Mine is an open residential institution, working with severe neuroses, some on the borderline of psychosis or psychopathy. In such a setting, the patients may display, in their most regressed moments, the milder forms of a disturbance in the sense of reality; in their daily behavior, they usually try to entertain, educate, and employ themselves in rational and useful ways; and in their best moments, they can be expected to be insightful and to do proficient and at times creative work. The hospital thus can be said to take a number of calculated risks, and to provide, on the other hand, special opportunities for the patient's abilities to work, to be active, and to share in social responsibilities. That a patient will fit into this setting has been established in advance during the "evaluation period." The patient's history has been taken in psychiatric interviews with him and perhaps with members of his family; he has been given a physical examination by a physician and has been confronted with standardized tests by psychologists who perform their work "blindly," that is, without knowledge of the patient's history; and finally, the results have been presented to the whole staff at a meeting, at the conclusion of which the patient himself was presented by the medical director, questioned by him and by other staff members, and assigned to "his therapist." Such preliminary screening has provided the therapist with an over-all diagnosis which defines a certain range of *expectable mental states*, indicating the patient's special danger points and his special prospects for improvement. Needless to say, not even the best preparation can quite predict what depths and heights may be reached once the therapeutic process gets under way.

The original test report had put the liability of our patient's state into these words: "The tests indicate border-line psychotic features in an inhibited, obsessive-compulsive character. However, the patient seems to be able to take spontaneously adequate distance from these border-line tendencies. He seems, at present, to be struggling to strengthen a rather precarious control over aggressive impulses, and probably feels a good deal of anxiety." The course of the treatment confirmed this and other test results. Thus, a dream-report of the kind just mentioned, in a setting of this kind, will first of all impress the clinical observer as a diagnostic sign. This is an "anxiety dream." Such a dream may happen to anybody, and a mild perseverance of the dream state into the day is not pathological as such. But this patient's dream appears to be only the visual center of a severe affective disturbance: no doubt if such a state were to persist, it could precipitate him into a generalized panic such as brought him to our clinic in the first place. The report of this horrible dream which intrudes itself on the patient's waking life now takes its place beside the data of the tests and the range and spectrum of the patient's moods and states as observed in the treatment, and shows him on the lowest level attained since admission, i.e., relatively closest to an *inability* "to take adequate distance from his borderline tendencies."

The first "prediction" to be made is whether this dream is the sign of an impending collapse, or, on the contrary, a potentially beneficial clinical crisis. The first would mean that the patient is slipping away from me and that I must think, as it were, of the emergency net; the second, that he is reaching out for me with an important message which I must try to understand and answer. I decided on the latter alternative. Although the patient acted as if he were close to a breakdown, I had the impression that, in fact, there was a challenge in all this, and a rather angry one. This impression was, to some extent, based on a comparison of the present hour and the previous one when the patient had seemed so markedly improved. Could it be that his unconscious had not been able to tolerate this very improvement? The paradox resolves itself if we consider that cure means the loss of the right to rely on therapy; for the cured patient, to speak with Saint Francis, would not so much seek to be loved as to love, and not so much to be consoled as to console, to the limit of his capacity. Does the dream-report communicate, protesting somewhat too loudly, that the patient is still sick? Is his dream sicker than the patient is? I can explain this tentative diagnostic conclusion only by presenting a number of inferences of a kind made very rapidly in a clinician's mind, and demonstrable only through an analysis of the patient's verbal and behavioral communications and of my own intellectual and affective reactions.

THE EXPERIENCED dream interpreter often finds himself "reading" a dream-report as a practitioner of medicine scans an X-ray. Especially in the cases of wordy or reticent patients or of lengthy case reports, a dream often lays bare the stark inner facts.

Let us first pay attention to the dream images. The main item is a large face without identifying features. There are no spoken words, and there is no motion. There are no people in the dream. Very apparent, then, are omissions. An experienced interpreter can state this on the basis of an implicit inventory of dream configurations against which he checks the individual dream production for present and absent dream configurations. This implicit inventory can be made explicit as I have myself tried to do in a publication reviewing Freud's classic first analysis of a "dream specimen." [2] The dream being discussed, then, is characterized by a significant omission of important items present in most dreams: motion, action, people, spoken words. All we have instead is a motionless image of a faceless face, which may or may not represent the patient's mother.

But in trying to understand what this image "stands for," the interpreter must abandon the classic scientific urge (leading to parsimonious explanation in some contexts but to "wild" interpretation in this one) to look for the one most plausible explanation. He must let his "free-floating" clinical attention and judgment lead him to all the *possible* faces which may be condensed in this one dream face and then decide what *probable meaning* may explain their combined presence. I will, then, proceed to relate the face in the dream to all the faces in my patient's hierarchy of significant persons, to my face as well as those of his mother and grandfather, to God's countenance as well as to the Medusa's grimace. Thus, the probable meaning of an empty and horrible face may gradually emerge.

First myself, then. The patient's facial and tonal expression reminded me of a series of critical moments during his treatment when he was obviously not quite sure that I was "all there" and apprehensive that I might disapprove of him and disappear in anger. This focused my attention on a question which the clinician must consider when faced with any of his patient's productions, namely, his own place in them.

While the psychotherapist should not force his way into the meanings of his patient's dream images, he does well to raise discreetly the masks of the various dream persons to see whether he can find his own face or person or role represented. Here the mask is an empty face, with plenty of horrible hair. My often unruly white hair surrounding a reddish face easily enters my patients' imaginative productions, either in the form of a benevolent Santa Claus or that of a threatening ogre. At that particular time, I had to consider another autobiographic item. In the third month of therapy, I had "abandoned" the patient to have an emergency operation which he, to use clinical shorthand, had ascribed to his evil eye. At the time of this dream-report I still was on occasion mildly uncomfortable—a matter which can never be hidden from such patients. A sensitive patient will, of course, be in conflict between his sympathy, which makes him want to take care of me, and his rightful claim that I should take care of him—for he feels that only the therapist's total presence can provide him with sufficient identity to weather his crises. I concluded that the empty face had something to do with a certain tenuousness in our relationship, and that one message of the dream might be something like this: "If I never know whether and when you think of yourself rather than attending to me, or when you will absent yourself, maybe die, *how can I have or gain what I need most—a coherent personality, an identity, a face?*"

Such an indirect message, however, even if understood as referring to the immediate present and to the therapeutic situation itself, always proves to be "overdetermined," that is, to consist of a *condensed code* transmitting a number of other messages, from other life situations, seemingly removed from the therapy. This we call *"transference."* Because the inference of a "mother transference" is by now an almost stereotyped requirement, and thus is apt to lead to faulty views concerning the relationship of past and present, I have postponed, but not discarded, a discussion of the connection between the patient's implied fear of "losing a face" with his remark that he was not sure the face was not his mother's. Instead, I put first his fear that he may yet lose himself by losing me too suddenly or too early.

CLINICAL WORK is always research in progress, and I would not be giving a full account of the clinician's pitfalls if I did not discuss in passing the fact that this patient's dream happened to fit especially well into my research at the time. This can be a mixed blessing for the therapeutic contract. A research-minded clinician—and one with literary ambitions, at that—must always take care lest his patients become footnotes to his favorite thesis or topic. I was studying in Pittsburgh and in Stockbridge the "identity crises" of a number of young people, college as well as seminary students, workmen and artists. My purpose was to delineate further a syndrome called *"identity-confusion,"* a term which describes the inability of young people in the late 'teens and early twenties to establish their station and vocation in life, and the tendency of some to develop apparently malignant symptoms and regressions.[3]

Such research must re-open rather than close questions of finalistic diagnosis. Perhaps there are certain stages in the life cycle when even seemingly malignant disturbances are more profitably treated as *aggravated life crises* rather than as diseases subject to routine psychiatric diagnosis. Here the clinician must be guided by the proposition that if he can hope to save only a small subgroup, or, indeed, only one patient, he must disregard existing statistical verdicts. For one new case, understood in new ways, will soon prove to be "typical" for a whole class of patients.

But any new diagnostic impression immediately calls for epidemiological considerations. What we have described as a therapeutic need in one patient, namely, to gain identity by claiming the total presence of his therapist, is identical with *the need of young people anywhere* for ideological affirmation. This need is aggravated in certain critical periods of history, when young people may try to find various forms of "confirmation" in groups that range from idealistic youth movements to criminal gangs.[4]

The young man in question was one among a small group of our patients who came from theological seminaries. He had developed his symptoms when attending a Protestant seminary in the Middle West where he was training for missionary work in Asia. He had not found the expected transformation in prayer, a matter which both for reasons of honesty and of inner need, he had taken more seriously than many successful believers. To him the wish to gaze through the glass darkly and to come "face to face" was a desperate need not easily satisfied in some modern seminaries. I need not remind you of the many references in the Bible to God's "making his face to shine upon" man, or God's face being turned away or being distant. The therapeutic theme inferred from the patient's report of an anxiety dream in which a face was horribly unrecognizable thus also seemed to echo relevantly this patient's religious scruples at the time of the appearance of psychiatric symptoms

—the common denominator being a *wish to break through to a provider of identity*.

This trend of thought, then, leads us from the immediate clinical situation (and a recognition of my face in the dream face) to the developmental crisis typical for the patient's age (and the possible meaning of facelessness as "identity-confusion"), to the vocational and spiritual crisis immediately preceding the patient's breakdown (and the need for a divine face, an existential recognition). The "buggy" in the dream will lead us a step further back into an earlier identity crisis—and yet another significant face.

The horse and buggy is, of course, an historical symbol of culture change. Depending on one's ideology, it is a derisive term connoting hopelessly old-fashioned ways, or it is a symbol of nostalgia for the good old days. Here we come to a trend in the family's history most decisive for the patient's identity crisis. The family came from Minnesota, where the mother's father had been a rural clergyman of character, strength, and communal esteem. Such grandfathers represent to many today a world of homogeneity in feudal values, "masterly and cruel with a good conscience, self-restrained and pious without loss of self-esteem." When the patient's parents had moved from the north country to then still smog-covered Pittsburgh, his mother especially had found it impossible to overcome an intense nostalgia for the rural ways of her youth. She had, in fact, imbued the boy with this nostalgia for a rural existence and had demonstrated marked disappointment when the patient, at the beginning of his identity crisis (maybe in order to cut through the family's cultural conflict), had temporarily threatened to become somewhat delinquent. The horse and buggy obviously is in greatest ideological as well as technological contrast to the modern means of locomotor acceleration, and, thus, all at once a symbol of changing times, of identity-confusion, and of cultural regression. Here the horrible motionlessness of the dream may reveal itself as an important configurational item, meaning something like being stuck in the middle of a world of competitive change and motion. And even as I inferred in my thoughts that the face sitting in the buggy must *also* represent the deceased grandfather's, also framed by white hair, the patient spontaneously embarked (as reported above) on a series of memories concerning the past when his grandfather had taken him by the hand to acquaint him with the technology of an old farm in Minnesota. Here the patient's vocabulary had become poetic, his description vivid, and he had seemed to be breaking through to a genuinely positive emotional experience. Yet as a reckless youngster he had defied this grandfather shortly before his death. Knowing this, I sympathized with his tearfulness which, nevertheless, remained strangely perverse, and sounded strangled by anger, as though he might be saying: "One must not promise a child such certainty, and then leave him."

Here it must be remembered that all "graduations" in human development mean the abandonment of a familiar position, and that all growth—that is, the kind of growth endangered in our patients—must come to terms with this fact.

We add to our previous inferences the assumption that the face in the dream (in a *condensation* typical for dream images) also "meant" the face of the grandfather who is now dead and whom as a rebellious youth the patient had defied. The immediate clinical situation, then, the history of the patient's breakdown and a certain period in his adolescence are all found to have a common denominator in the idea that the patient wishes to *base his future sanity on a countenance of wisdom and firm identity* while, in all instances, he seems to fear that his anger may have destroyed, or may yet destroy, such resources. The patient's desperate insistence on finding security in prayer and, in fact, in missionary work, and yet his failure to find peace in these endeavors belongs in this context.

It may be necessary to assure you at this point that it is the failure of religious endeavor, not religiosity or the need for reverence and service, which is thereby explained. In fact, there is every reason to assume that the development of a sense of fidelity and the capacity to give and to receive it in a significant setting is a condition for a young adult's health, and of a young patient's recovery.

THE THEME of the horse and buggy as a rural symbol served to establish a possible connection between the nostalgic mother and her dead father; and we now finally turn our attention to the fact that the patient, half-denying what he was half-suggesting, said, "I am not sure it wasn't my mother." Here the most repetitious complaint of the whole course of therapy must be reviewed. While the grandfather's had been, all in all, the most consistently reassuring countenance in the patient's life, the mother's pretty, soft, and loving face had since earliest childhood been marred in the patient's memory and imagination by moments when she seemed absorbed and distorted by strong and painful emotions. The tests, given before any history-taking, had picked out the following theme: "The mother-figure appears in the Thematic Apperception Tests as one who seeks to control her son by her protectiveness of him, and by 'self-pity' and demonstrations of her frailty at any aggressive act on his part. She is, in the stories, 'frightened' at any show of rebelliousness, and content only when the son is passive and compliant. There appears to be considerable aggression, probably partly conscious, toward this figure." And indeed, it was with anger as well as with horror that the patient would repeatedly describe the mother of his memory as utterly exasperated, and this at those times when he had been too rough, too careless, too stubborn, or too persistent.

We are not concerned here with accusing this actual mother of having behaved this way; we can only be sure that she appeared this way in certain retrospective moods of the patient. Such memories are typical for a certain class of patients, and the question whether this is so because they have in common a certain type of mother or share a typical reaction to their mothers, or both, occupies the thinking of clinicians. At any rate many of these patients are deeply, if often unconsciously, convinced that they have caused a basic disturbance in their mothers. Often, in our time, when corporal punishment and severe scolding have become less fashionable, parents resort to the seemingly less cruel means of presenting themselves as deeply hurt by the child's willfulness. The "violated" mother thus tends to appear more prominently in images of guilt. In some cases this becomes an obstacle in the resolution of adolescence—as if a fundamental and yet quite impossible restitution were a condition for adulthood. It is in keeping with this trend that the patients under discussion here, young people who in late adolescence face a breakdown on the borderline of psychosis, all prove to be partially regressed to the earliest task in life, namely, the acquisition of a sense of basic trust strong enough to balance that sense of basic mistrust to which newborn man (most dependent of all young animals and yet endowed with fewer inborn instinctive regulations) is subject in his infancy. We all relive earlier and earliest stages of our existence in dreams, in artistic experience, and in religious devotion, only to emerge refreshed and invigorated. These patients, however, experience such partial regression in a lonely, sudden, and intense fashion, and most of all with a sense of irreversible doom. This, too, is in this dream.

The mother's veiled presence in the dream points to a complete omission in all this material: there is no father either in the dream or in the associated themes. The patient's father images became dominant in a later period of the treatment and proved most important for the patient's eventual solution of his spiritual and vocational problems. From this we can dimly surmise that in the present hour the grandfather "stands for" the father.

On the other hand, the recognition of the mother's countenance in the empty dream face and its surrounding slimy hair suggests the discussion of a significant symbol. Did not Freud explain the Medusa, the angry face with snake-hair and an open mouth, as a *symbol of the feminine void*, and an expression of the masculine horror of femininity? It is true that some of the patient's memories and associations (reported in other sessions in connection with the mother's emotions) could be easily traced to infantile observations and ruminations concerning "female trouble," pregnancy, and post-partum upsets. Facelessness, in this sense, can also mean inner void, and (from a male point of view) "castration." Does it, then, or does it not contradict Freudian symbolism if I emphasize in this equally horrifying but entirely empty face a representation of facelessness, of loss of face, of lack of identity? In the context of the "classical" interpretation, the dream image would be primarily symbolic of a sexual idea which is to be warded off, in ours a representation of a danger to the continuous existence of individual identity. Theoretical considerations would show that these interpretations do not exclude each other. In this case a possible controversy is superseded by the clinical consideration that a symbol to be interpreted must first be shown to be immediately relevant. It would be futile to use sexual symbolism dogmatically when acute interpersonal needs can be discerned as dominant in strongly concordant material. The sexual symbolism of this dream was taken up in due time, when it reappeared in another context, namely that of manhood and sexuality, and revealed the bisexual confusion inherent in all identity conflict.

TRACING ONE MAIN THEME of the dream retrospectively, we have recognized it in four periods of the patient's life—all four premature graduations which left him with anger and fear over what he was to abandon rather than with the anticipation of greater freedom and more genuine identity: the present treatment—and the patient's fear that by some act of horrible anger (on his part or on mine or both) he might lose me and thus his chance to regain his identity through trust in me; his immediately preceding religious education—and his abortive attempt at finding through prayer that "presence" which would cure his inner void; his earlier youth—and his hope to gain strength, peace, and identity by identifying himself with his grandfather; and, finally, early childhood—and his desperate wish to keep alive in himself the charitable face of his mother in order to overcome fear, guilt, and anger over her emotions. Such redundancy points to a central theme which, once found, gives added meaning to all the associated material. The theme is: "Whenever I begin to have faith in somebody's strength and love, some angry and sickly emotions pervade the relationship, and I end up mistrusting, empty, and a victim of anger and despair."

You may be getting a bit tired of the clinician's habit of speaking for the patient, of putting into his mouth inferences which, so it would seem, he could get out of him for the asking. The clinician, however, has no right to test his reconstructions until his trial formulations have combined into a comprehensive interpretation which feels right to him, and which promises, when appropriately verbalized, to feel right to the patient. When this point is reached, the clinician usually finds himself compelled to speak, in order to help the patient in verbalizing his affects and images in a more communicative manner, and to communicate his own impressions.

If according to Freud a successful dream is an attempt at representing a wish as fulfilled, the attempted and miscarried fulfillment in this dream is that of finding a face with a lasting identity. If an anxiety dream startling the dreamer out of his sleep is a symptom of a derailed wish-fulfillment, the central theme just formulated indicates at least one inner disturbance which caused the miscarriage of basic trust in infancy.

It seemed important to me that my communication should

include an explicit statement of my emotional response to the dream-report. Patients of the type of our young man, still smarting in his twenties under what he considered his mother's strange emotions in his infancy, can learn to delineate social reality and to tolerate emotional tension only if the therapist can juxtapose his own emotional reactions to the patient's emotions. Therefore, as I reviewed with the patient some of what I have put before you, I also told him without rancor, but not without some honest indignation, that my response to his account had included a feeling of being attacked. I explained that he had worried me, had made me feel pity, had touched me with his memories, and had challenged me to prove, all at once, the goodness of mothers, the immortality of grandfathers, my own perfection, and God's grace.

The words used in an interpretation, however, are hard to remember and when reproduced or recorded often sound as arbitrary as any private language developed by two people in the course of an intimate association. But whatever is said, a therapeutic interpretation, while brief and simple in form, should encompass a *unitary theme* such as I have put before you, a theme common at the same time to a dominant trend in the patient's relation to the therapist, to a significant portion of his symptomatology, to an important conflict of his childhood, and to corresponding facets of his work and love life. This sounds more complicated than it is. Often, a very short and casual remark proves to have encompassed all this; and the trends *are* (as I must repeat in conclusion) very closely related to each other in the patient's own struggling mind, for which the traumatic past is of course a present frontier, perceived as acute conflict. Such an interpretation, therefore, joins the patient's and the therapist's modes of problem-solving.

Therapists of different temperament and of various persuasions differ as to what constitutes an interpretation: an impersonal and authoritative explanation, a warm and parental suggestion, an expansive sermon or a sparse encouragement to go on and see what comes up next. The intervention in this case, however, highlights one methodological point truly unique to clinical work, namely, the disposition of the clinician's "mixed" feelings, his emotions and opinions. The evidence is not "all in" if he does not succeed in using his own emotional responses during a clinical encounter as an evidential source and as a guide in intervention, instead of putting them aside with a spurious claim to unassailable objectivity. It is here that the prerequisite of the therapist's own psychoanalytic treatment as a didactic experience proves itself essential, for the personal equation in the observer's emotional response is as important in psychotherapy as that of the senses in the laboratory. Repressed emotions easily hide themselves in the therapist's most stubborn blind spots.

I do not wish to make too much of this, but I would suggest in passing that some of us have, to our detriment, embraced an objectivity which can only be maintained with self-deception. If "psychoanalyzed" man learns to recognize the fact that even his previously repudiated or denied impulses may be "right" in their refusal to be submerged without a trace (the traces being his symptoms), so he may also learn that his strongest ethical judgments are right in being persistent even if modern life may not consider it intelligent or advantageous to feel strongly about such matters. Any psychotherapist, then, who throws out his ethical sentiments with his irrational moral anger, deprives himself of a principal tool of his clinical perception. For even as our sensuality sharpens our awareness of the orders of nature, so our indignation, admitted and scrutinized for flaws of sulkiness and self-indulgence, is, in fact, an important tool both of therapy and of theory. It adds to the investigation of what, indeed, has happened to sick individuals a suggestion of where to look for those epidemiological factors that should and need not happen to anybody. But this means that we somehow harbor a model of man which could serve as a scientific basis for the postulation of an ethical relation of the generations to each other; and that we are committed to this whether or not we abrogate our partisanship in particular systems of morality.

A certain combination of available emotion and responsive thought, then, marks a therapist's style and is expressed in minute variations of facial expression, posture, and tone of voice. The core of a therapeutic intervention at its most decisive thus defies any attempt at a definitive account. This difficulty is not overcome by the now widespread habit of advocating a "human," rather than a "technical" encounter. Even humanness can be a glib "posture," and the time may come when we need an injunction against the use in vain of this word "human," too.

WHAT DO WE EXPECT the patient to contribute to the closure of our evidence? What tells us that our interpretation was "right," and, therefore, proves the evidence to be as conclusive as it can be in our kind of work? The simplest answer is that this particular patient was amused, delighted, and encouraged when I told him of my thoughts and my feelings over his unnecessary attempts to burden me with a future which he could well learn to manage—a statement which was not meant to be a therapeutic "suggestion" or a clinical slap on the back, but was based on what I knew of his inner resources as well as of the use he made of the opportunities offered in our clinical community. The patient left the hour—to which he had come with a sense of dire disaster—with a broad smile and obvious encouragement. Otherwise, only the future would show whether the process of recovery had been advanced by this hour.

But then, one must grant that the dream experience itself was a step in the right direction. I would not want to leave you with the impression that I accused the patient of pretending illness, or that I belittled his dream as representing sham despair. On the contrary, I acknowledged that he had taken a real chance with himself and with me. Under my protection and the hospital's he had hit bottom by chancing a repetition of his original breakdown. He had gone to the very border of unreality and had gleaned from it a highly condensed and seemingly anarchic image. Yet that image, while experienced as a symptom, was in fact a kind of creation, or at any rate a condensed and highly meaningful communication and challenge, to which my particular clinical theory had made me receptive. A sense of mutuality and reality was thus restored, reinforced by the fact that while accepting his transferences as meaningful, I had refused to become drawn into them. I had played neither mother, grandfather, nor God (this is the hardest), but had offered him my help as defined by my professional status in attempting to understand what was behind his helplessness. By relating the fact that his underlying anger aroused mine, and that I could say so without endangering either myself or him, I could show him that in his dream he had also confronted anger in the image of a Medusa—a Gorgon which, neither of us being a hero, we could yet slay together.

The proof of the correctness of our inference does, of course, not always lie in the patient's immediate assent. I have, in fact, indicated how this very dream experience followed an hour in which the patient had assented too much. Rather, the proof lies in the way in which the communication between therapist and patient "keeps moving," leading to new and surprising insights and to the patient's greater assumption of responsibility for himself. In this he is helped, if hospitalized, by the social influences of the "therapeutic community," and by well-guided work activities—all of which would have to be taken into account, if I were concerned here with the nature of *the therapeutic process* rather than with that of clinical evidence. But it is important to remember that only in a favorable social setting, be it the private patient's private life or the hospitalized patient's planned community, can the two main therapeutic agents described here function fully: the insight gained into the pathogenic past, and the convincing presence of a therapeutic relationship which bridges past and future.

I MAY NOW confess that the initial invitation really requested me to tell you "how a *good* clinician works." I have replaced this embarrassing little word with dots until now when I can make it operational. It is a mark of the good clinician that much can go on in him without clogging his communication at the moment of therapeutic intervention, when only the central theme may come to his awareness. Since a clinician's identity as a worker is based (as is anybody else's) on decisive learning experiences during the formative years of his first acquaintance with the field of his choice, he cannot avoid carrying with him some traditional formulations which may range in their effect from ever helpful clarifications to burdening dogmatisms. In a good clinician, such formulations have become a matter of implicit insight and of a style of action. On the other hand, he must also be able to call his ruminations to explicit awareness when professional conferences permit their being spelled out—for how else could such thinking be disciplined, shared and taught? Such sharing and teaching, in turn, if it is to transcend clinical impressionism, presupposes a communality of conceptual approaches. I cannot give you today more than a suggestion that there is a systematic relationship between clinical observation on the one hand and, on the other, such conceptual points of view as Freud has introduced into psychiatry: a *structural* point of view denoting a kind of anatomy of the mind, a *dynamic* point of view denoting a kind of physiology of mental forces, a *genetic* point of view reconstructing the growth of the mind and the stages marking its strengths and its dangers, and finally, an *adaptive* point of view.[5] But even as such propositions are tested on a wide front of inquiry (from the direct observation of children and perception experiments to "metapsychological" discussion), it stands to reason that clinical evidence is characterized by an immediacy which transcends formulations ultimately derived from mechanistic patterns of thought.

The "points of view" introduced into psychiatry and psychology by Freud are, at this time, subject to a strange fate. No doubt, they were the bridges by which generations of medical clinicians could apply their anatomical, physiological, and pathological modes of thinking to the workings of the mind. Probably also, the neurological basis of behavior was thus fruitfully related to other determinants; I myself cannot judge the fate of Freud's neurological assumptions as such. A transfer of concepts from one field to another has in other fields led to revolutionary clarifications and yet eventually also to a necessary transcendence of the borrowed concepts by newer and more adequate ones. In psychoanalysis, the fate of the "points of view" was pre-ordained: since on their medical home ground they were based on visible facts such as organs and functions, in the study of the mind they sooner or later served improper reifications, as though libido or the death-instinct or the ego really existed. Freud was sovereignly aware of this danger, but always willing to learn by giving a mode of thought free reign to see to what useful model it might lead. He also had the courage, the authority, and the inner consistency to reverse such a direction when it became useless or absurd. Generations of clinical practitioners cannot be expected to be equally detached or authoritative. Thus it cannot be denied that in much clinical literature the clinical evidence secured with the help of inferences based on Freud's theories has been increasingly used and slanted to verify the original theories. This, in turn, could only lead to a gradual estrangement between theory and clinical observation.

I should, therefore, say explicitly which of the traditional psychoanalytic concepts have remained intrinsic to my clinical way of thinking. I would say that I have to assume that the patient is (to varying degrees) *unconscious* of the meaning which I discern in his communications, and that I am helping him by making fully conscious what may be totally repressed, barely conscious, or simply cut off from communication. By doing so, however, I take for granted an effective wish on his part (with my help) to see, feel and speak more clearly. I would also assume a *regressive trend*, a going back to earlier failures in order to solve the past along with the present. In doing so, however, I would not give the past a kind of fatalistic dominance over the present: for the temporal rear can be brought up only where the present finds consolidation. I would also acknowledge the power of *transference*, i.e., the patient's transfer to me of significant problems in his past dealings with the central people in his life; but I would know that only by playing my role as a new person in his present stage of life can I clarify the inappropriateness of his transferences from the past. In this past, I would consider libidinal attachments and relationships of dependence and of abandonment of paramount importance: but I would assume, in line with everything that we have learned about human development, that these relationships were not disturbed only by a *libidinal disbalance*. Such disbalance, in fact, is part of a *missed mutuality* which kept the child from realizing his potential strength even as the parent was hindered in living up to his potentialities by the very failure of mutuality in relation to this child. You will note, then, that in naming the rock-bottom concepts of repression and regression, transference and libido, I have tried to keep each linked with the observation and experience of the clinical encounter as a new event in the patient's life history. You would find other clinical workers similarly groping for a position which permits them to honor the therapeutic contract as they use and advance the theory of the field. At the end, the therapist's chosen intervention and the patient's reactions to it are an integral part of the evidence provided in the thera-

peutic encounter. It is from such experience that the psychotherapist goes back to his drawing board, back to his models of
the mind, to the blueprints of intervention and to his plans for
the wider application of clinical insight.

I HAVE GIVEN YOU an example which ends on a convincing
note, leaving both the patient and the practitioner with the
feeling that they are a pretty clever pair. If it were always required to clinch a piece of clinical evidence in this manner, we
should have few convincing examples. To tell the truth, I think
that we often learn more from our failures—if indeed we can
manage to review them in the manner here indicated. But I
hope to have demonstrated that there is enough method in our
work to force favorite assumptions to become probable inferences by cross-checking the patient's diagnosis and what we
know of his type of illness and state of physical health; his stage
of development and what we know of the "normative" crisis
of his age-group; the co-ordinates of his social position and
what we know of the chances of a man of his type, intelligence, and education in the social actuality of our time. This
may be hard to believe unless one has heard an account of a
series of such encounters as I have outlined here, the series
being characterized by a progressive or regressive shift in all
the areas mentioned: such is the evidence used in our clinical
conferences and seminars.

Much of clinical training, in fact, consists of the charting
of such series. In each step, our auxiliary methods must help us
work with reasonable precision and with the courage to re-
vise our assumptions and our techniques systematically, if and
when the clinical evidence should show that we overestimated
or underestimated the patient or ourselves, the chances waiting for him in his environment, or the usefulness of our particular theory.

In order to counteract any subjectivity and selectivity, whole treatments are now being sound-filmed so that qualified secondary observers can follow the procedure and have certain items repeated many times over, sometimes in slow motion. This will be important in some lines of research, and advantageous in training. Yet, it confronts a second observer or a series of observers with the task of deciding on the basis of their reactions, whether or not they agree with the judgments of the original observer made on the basis of his unrecordable reactions. Nor does the nature of clinical evidence change in such new developments as group-psychotherapy, where a therapist faces a group of patients and they face one another as well, permitting a number of combinations and variations of the basic elements of a clinical encounter. Clinical evidence, finally, will be decisively clarified, but not changed in nature, by a sharpened awareness (such as now emanates from sociological studies) of the psychotherapist's as well as the patient's position in society and history.

The relativity implicit in clinical work may, to some, militate against its scientific value. Yet, I suspect, that this very relativity, truly acknowledged, will make the clinicians better companions of today's and tomorrow's scientists than did the attempts to reduce the study of the human mind to a science identical with traditional natural science. I, therefore, have restricted myself to giving an operational introduction to the clinician's basic view which asserts that scientists may learn about the nature of things by finding out what they can do *to* them, but that the clinician can learn of the true nature of man only in the attempt to do something *for* and *with* him. I have focused, therefore, on the way in which clinical evidence is grounded in the study of what is *unique* to the *individual* case —including the psychotherapist's involvement. Such uniqueness, however, would not stand out without the background of that other concern, which I have neglected here, namely the study of what is *common* to verifiable *classes* of cases.

III

Identity and Uprootedness
in Our Time

The first two lectures dealt with psychoanalysis as grounded in the psychotherapeutic observation of the individual who becomes pathologically "upset" in the course of his life. The third applies clinical insight to a whole class of sufferers who are uprooted by historical fate. This address was given before a plenary session of the World Federation of Mental Health, held at the University of Vienna, in 1959. This session followed intensive discussions of the plight of emigrants and refugees all over the world.

THE MENTAL HEALTH of individuals torn away from their homes, their work, and their country in forced migration has repeatedly been a special concern of international meetings. Being an immigrant myself (like so many of my countrymen and most of their parents or grandparents), I may begin by confessing a symptomatic bit of everyday pathology. We all know the experience of finding ourselves whistling or humming a melody, first without being especially aware of it, but then with an obsessiveness that can become a mild state of malaise—for ourselves as well as for our neighbors. Often we can release ourselves (and them) from such tyranny only after we have realized the message in the melody.

In the last few weeks I have been haunted by Dvořák's *New World* Symphony; and when I stopped and listened it was not hard to perceive that I was arming myself for the moment when I would have to speak about identity and uprootedness. The *New World* Symphony, that blend of American horizons and European valleys served as a bright reassurance against the scruples and symptoms attending my own emigration. But most of all, I think it was to reassert my status as an American *immigrant*. This term soon after my migration gave way to that of *refugee*—even as such terms as *settler* or *pioneer* had already become mythological, giving way to *migrant* and *itinerant*.

The little prefix "in" has a special significance in the termini of transmigration: it can, indeed, make "a world of difference." As in the contemporary Israeli term "ingathering" in-migration can connote the promise of maternal acceptance, a promise to the voluntary newcomer that he will find new roots in a new soil, and a new identity encouraged by the receiving country's active wish to absorb him. *Sovereign and mutual choice* is the tenor of the *New World* Symphony: the sovereign choice of one who decides to migrate, and the mutual choice of new and old settlers. But it is clear that this symphony, in view of the grim and complex facts of all immigration, is also an historical lullaby. And repetitious melodies often are, I would think, anachronistic lullabies.

First a word, then, on the decision to migrate. Daniel Lerner recently asked Turkish villagers where, if they had to emigrate, they would go.[1] Many were too horrified even to think of alternatives: it would seem "worse than death," they said. The early American immigrants, however, did make that one desperate decision to pick themselves up, as it were, by their roots—a decision which eventually forced them to create a new "way of life," that is, new sources and patterns of personal and industrial energy and a new ideological orientation. They chose change, to actively transplant old roots, and then were forced to find new roots in Change itself. They took a chance and then had to revere Chance, even where unlimited opportunities for the few meant drabness and oblivion for the rest. They created a new elite out of the types of men who fit this new world. While the women insisted on the three R's, the men were bent on the three Ch's—Change, Chance, Choice

—the basis of an ideology, which, at the time of my arrival (it was the period of the New Deal), experienced a late flowering.

With the approach of World War II the new term "refugee" became dominant, and I would say that it was indicative not only of a new attitude among the now sedentary Americans, but also among the newcomers. Having lived through or barely escaped unspeakable danger before embarkation, most refugees nevertheless had at their disposal, on arrival in America, all the choices and all the chances which earlier newcomers had had—and often very much more. Yet many of them initially refused to be submerged in the futuristic ideology of immigration, holding on, instead, to the world that had disowned them. A few angrily insisted they had inside information that the Nazis already had a foothold in Texas and were forming S.S. battalions. Beset by the traumatic fact that the only alternative to their migration would have been annihilation by their own countrymen, they had learned to depend on an element of persecution without which life was unpredictable, and thus, in a way, less safe.

In these and other ways many of us have ourselves met with the symptoms of unrootedness and resettlement. It is now our task to help clarify a few universal mental mechanisms in the adaptation of the trans-migrant. I cannot offer my contribution to these problems, however, without one word of remembrance for those who could not join us in migration: the dead. The very worst conditions of migration would yet have offered them their naked life, and a flicker of hope in a possible humanity. But to them even flight was denied; and our image of man must forever include the hell which was their last experience on earth.

TRANSMIGRATIONS, like all catastrophes and collective crises, produce new traumatic world images, and seem to demand the sudden assumption of new and often transitory identities. What motivates and moves the transmigrant; how he has been excluded or has excluded himself from his previous home; how he has been transported or has chosen to traverse the distance between home and destination; and how he has been kept or has kept himself separate, or has been absorbed and has involved himself in his new setting—these are the situational determinants. They do not account in themselves, however, for the second set of determinants, clarified by Sigmund Freud. Freud speaks of a mental mechanism of "turning passive into active," a mechanism central to the maintenance of man's individuality, for it enables him to maintain and regain in this world of contending forces an individual position marked by *centrality*, *wholeness*, and *initiative*. You may suspect that these are the attributes of what we call identity.

There is a saying which is considered typical of the American pioneer: "When you see the smoke from your neighbor's chimney, it is time to move on." It illustrates the stubborn habituation to a pattern of active mastery over an originally compelling and confining fate: one does not wait, one moves of one's own accord. The psychological counterpart of this— even if the exact opposite in overt pattern—is a remark addressed to me by an old Chassidic Jew in the streets of Jerusalem: "An American?" he asked. I nodded and he looked into my eyes with sympathy, almost pity. "*We* know where we are, and *here* we stay." With quiet triumph he added: "*Schlusspunkt*"—an emphatic "period."

You can actively flee, then, and you can actively stay put; you even can (as Louise Pinsky said about some youths in the European underground) "actively hide." [2] On the other hand, you can feel uprooted if you are not permitted to roam perpetually, as witness the remnants of the American Plains Indians, who, on their own prairie, were forced to abandon nomadic life. Long after the government had settled them in frame houses, they asked for trailers to live in. Not permitted to perambulate at will, they developed in their actions and in their speech that same intangible drag of a slow-motion picture which is typical of depressed individuals and which Dr. Bakis reports in the inmates of an internment camp. [3] The tribal identity of the nomadic hunters had developed its roots in perpetual motion. I have described how the remnants of the tribe, forced into sedentary life, seemed to behave like helpless patients. [4]

Patienthood, then, is a condition of inactivation. *Agens* is the opposite of *patiens* and we will use this opposition here in order to give additional meaning to such terms as "passive" and "active," and to free them from such connotations as aggressive and submissive, male and female. *Patiens*, then, would denote a state of being exposed from within or from without to superior forces which cannot be overcome without prolonged patience or energetic and redeeming help; while *agens* connotes an inner state of being unbroken in initiative and of acting in the service of a cause which sanctions this initiative. You will see immediately that the stage of *agens* is what all clients, or patients, in groups or alone are groping for and need our help to achieve. But it is also clear that we are not speaking of a condition of overt activity, but of an inner state which we conceptualize as active tension in the ego.

LET ME CONTRAST to the old Chassid in Jerusalem, who stayed with a vengeance (*Schlusspunkt*), an old Jew from the American Middle West, who began to wander when he became a patient in the sense of a medical client. Highly successful in his business career, he was ready to retire to Southern California, never to suffer again the rigors of the North and the commercial pressure of metropolitan life. As he was liquidating his routine work, however, he began to suffer unbearable pain all over his chest, a pain for which his doctors could find no organic basis. The man took to walking about town, not with an ordinary cane but a long stick; the neighbors began to refer to him as the Wandering Jew. He confided a recurrent dream to his doctor: he was back at home by a wide Russian river, where his father had built boats to be floated down-river fully loaded, and sold in some harbor. But in the man's dream all his father's half-finished and unloaded boats were torn from their moorings and were inexorably drifting down-river.

To interpret this dream one psychosocial and one psychosomatic fact must suffice. This man had left home when he was thirteen, the age of confirmation; and the area of his chest pain proved to coincide with that once covered by a ritual undergarment which he had discarded when he had left home. At the moment of having *arrived* in life, this man suffered (and suffered fatally) from guilt over the youthful decision to *leave*. In his manhood he had become a great benefactor of synagogues and charities, yet deep down he felt only like one of his father's unfinished boats, torn from its moorings too early, and unfaithful to its "maker." You may know how difficult it is to help an old man whose patienthood has thus become his individualized passion. And indeed, this man died not long after his dream, from a somatic cause unrelated to his chest pain. But not infrequently in the aged, a kind of integrity struggle seems to take hold of an as yet undefined somatic condition in order to express an old identity failure, which has left unsolved some pervading guilt. For there is guilt in the dream's underlying question: who untied the boats—and to what end? Beyond this you will recognize in the symbolism of ropes a variation on the theme of roots which pervades our imagery on the subject of transmigration. There roots are torn out or are brought along, dry up in transit or are kept moist and alive, find an appropriate soil, or fail to take hold and wither.

A case of this kind combines elements of patienthood which include our work of individual cure and of social rehabilitation. The old man stands midway between those who are driven by inner conflicts or unmanageable drives (the *Getriebenen*, the driven ones) and those who have *been* driven from soil and home (the *Vertriebenen*, the expelled ones). Their common symptoms betray a common state in their ego which has lost active mastery and the nourishing exchange of community life. On one end of a series, then, are those who are driven by unmanageable impulses: they, too, feel "upset" and "unsettled." In the middle are those who are coerced by their inner compulsions: they, too, "persecute themselves." On the other end of the series are those arrested, driven away and driven out by persecuting forces. The symptoms displayed, either transitorily or chronically, by all these classes of victims demonstrate how the ego, in its effort to adapt to overpowering odds, unhesitatingly arms itself against the various driving, compelling, and persecuting forces, forming of all a common enemy in order to establish a united, defense. Thus, the persecutor outside finds an ally in the hidden inner persecutor to create an increased sense of worthlessness where the situation would call for cunning and resolution. Inner guilt will accept as inexorable what should and could be resisted or managed. Home-sickness turns into a self-accusation for having abandoned a land one was actually driven from. In other words, the ego's capacity for initiative is inactivated by a conspiracy of historical fate and personal history. In all of this, however, we recognize remnants of the individual's need (central to the functioning of his ego) to experience fate as something which he chose and in which he was active, even if this means to have chosen or caused, invited or accepted annihilation or persecution and exile. We can observe this, I believe, particularly clearly in those who have become mere serial numbers in a mass of dislocated individuals and who develop delusions of being persecuted even by those who would rehabilitate them. If you have forgotten how to trust, you may be driven to cultivate active mistrust and insist defiantly that everybody is against you.

Thus the problems of patienthood caused by outer and by inner conditions overlap, and I submit that they overlap as well in the problem of identity. This term, however, is so widely used in our country that it is as important to say what it does *not* imply, as it is to delineate what it may mean in this context.

IN THE CASE of the old man I spoke of a *confirmation* unfulfilled in his youth, and we should, for a moment, dwell on the fact that there is a "natural" period of uprootedness in human life: adolescence. Like a trapeze artist, the young person in the middle of vigorous motion must let go of his safe hold on childhood and reach out for a firm grasp on adulthood, depending for a breathless interval on a relatedness between the past and the future, and on the reliability of those he must let go of, and those who will "receive" him. Whatever combination of drives and defenses, of sublimations and capacities has emerged from the young individual's childhood must now make sense in view of his concrete opportunities in work and in love; what the individual has learned to see in himself must now coincide with the expectations and recognitions which others bestow on him; whatever values have become meaningful to him must now match some universal significance.

Identity formation thus goes beyond the process of *identifying oneself with* others in the one-way fashion described in earlier psychoanalysis. It is a process based on a heightened cognitive and emotional capacity to *let oneself be identified* as a circumscribed individual in relation to a predictable universe which transcends the circumstances of childhood. Identity thus is not the sum of childhood identifications, but rather a new combination of old and new identification fragments. For this very reason societies *confirm* an individual at this time in all kinds of ideological frameworks and assign roles and tasks to him in which he can *recognize* himself and *feel recognized*. Ritual confirmations, initiations, and indoctrinations only enhance an indispensable process by which healthy societies bestow traditional strength on the new generation and thereby bind to themselves the strength of youth. Societies thus verify the new individual and are themselves historically verified, for the individual is induced to put at the disposal of societal processes that "conflict-free" energy which he was able to save up, as it were, from his infantile conflicts. Such an intricate process, however, which has evolved both with the evolution of the individual and of society cannot be fostered by synthetic values, nor can the product be confirmed with empty ceremony: here the weakened creeds of the West and the manufactured ideologies of the Communist world may meet a common obstacle.

It is here that we should pay at least passing attention to those young people who choose or are drafted into the movements and organizations which *do* the expelling. As unconditionally as we hate the leaders who use them, we must never stop inquiring by what inner mechanisms the young can be made to participate fanatically in acts of cowardly extermination. The answer is that they, too, are uprooted—as adolescents, and as adolescing members of nations and classes which are denied the promise of a certain wholeness of national and economic identity, and that thus they grasp at, or let themselves be grasped by, what one may call totalistic ideologies.

Young people must become whole people in their own right, and this during a developmental stage characterized by a diversity of changes in physical growth, in genital maturation, and in social awareness. The wholeness to be achieved at this stage I have called a sense of inner identity. The young person, in order to experience wholeness, must feel a progressive continuity between that which he has come to be during the long years of childhood and that which he promises to become in the anticipated future; between that which he conceives himself to be and that which he perceives others to see in him and to expect of him. Individually speaking, identity includes, but is more than the sum of, all the successive identifications of those earlier years when the child wanted to be, and often was forced to become, like the people he depended on. Identity is a unique product, which now meets a crisis to be solved only in new identifications with age-mates and with leader figures outside of the family. The adolescent search for a new and yet a reliable identity can perhaps best be seen in the persistent endeavor to define, to overdefine, and to redefine oneself and each other in often ruthless comparison; while the search for reliable alignments can be seen in the restless testing of the newest in possibilities and the oldest in values. Where the resulting self-definition, for personal or for collective reasons, becomes too difficult, a sense of role confusion results: the youth counterpoints rather than synthesizes his sexual, ethnic, occupational, and typological alternatives and is often driven to decide definitely and totally for one side or the other.

In discussing identity, I have used the terms "wholeness" and "totality." Both mean entireness; yet let me underscore their differences. Wholeness seems to connote an assembly of parts, even quite diversified parts, that enter into fruitful association and organization. This concept is most strikingly expressed in such terms as wholeheartedness, wholemindedness, wholesomeness, and the like. As a *Gestalt*, then, wholeness emphasizes a sound, organic, progressive mutuality between diversified functions and parts within an entirety, the boundaries of which are open and fluent. Totality, on the contrary, evokes a *Gestalt* in which an absolute boundary is emphasized: given a certain arbitrary delineation, nothing that belongs inside must be left outside, nothing that must be outside can be tolerated inside. A totality is as absolutely inclusive as it is utterly exclusive: whether or not the category-to-be-made-absolute is a logical one, and whether or not the parts really have, so to speak, a yearning for one another.

It is, then, the psychological need for a totality without further choice or alternation, even if it implies the abandonment of a much desired wholeness, which I would invite you to consider. To say it with one sentence: When the human being, because of accidental or developmental shifts, loses an essential wholeness, he restructures himself and the world by taking recourse to what we may call *totalism*. It would be wise to abstain from considering this a merely regressive or infantile mechanism. It is an alternate, if more primitive, way of dealing with experience, and thus has, at least in transitory states, a certain adjustment and survival value. It belongs to normal psychology.

True identity, however, depends on the support which the young individual receives from the collective sense of identity characterizing the social groups significant to him: his class, his nation, his culture. Where historical and technological developments severely encroach upon deeply rooted or strongly emerging identities (i.e., agrarian, feudal, patrician) on a large scale, youth feels endangered, individually and collectively, whereupon it becomes ready to support doctrines offering a total immersion in a synthetic identity (extreme nationalism, racism, or class consciousness) and a collective condemnation of a totally stereotyped enemy of the new identity. The fear of loss of identity which fosters such indoctrination contributes significantly to that mixture of righteousness and criminality which, under totalitarian conditions, becomes available for organized terror and for the establishment of major industries of extermination. Since conditions undermining a sense of identity also fixate older individuals on adolescent alternatives, a great number of adults fall in line or are paralyzed in their resistance.

Here a futile cycle of evil comes to be established. For even where totalitarian crime may seem, indeed, to "pay" in success and self-aggrandizement, the totalistic orientation cannot lead to that relative wholeness of experience by which cultures as well as individuals live. But neither can those who overcome the persecutor gain peace from mere acts of righteous vengeance, by which they attempt to eliminate, along with the criminals, the memory of the crime. In view of the means of destruction at the disposal of leaders of the future, our historical memory is in obvious need of a more responsible assessment of the evil that threatens whenever new generations are denied any other identity but that of self-assertion through total repudiation.[5]

UNDER CERTAIN personal and cultural conditions *developmental crises* can occur precociously. Anna Freud and Sophie Dann have demonstrated the precocious development of a social conscience in the form of an excessive and maladaptive peer solidarity in concentration-camp children.[6] The identity crisis, too, can come too early. Margaret Macfarland of the Arsenal Nursery School in Pittsburgh told me of a four-year-old Negro girl who used to stand in front of a mirror and scrub her skin with soap. When gently diverted from this she began to scrub the mirror. Finally, when induced to paint instead, she first angrily filled sheets of paper with the colors brown and black. But then she brought to the teacher what she called "a really *good* picture." The teacher at first could see only a white sheet, until she looked more closely and saw that the little girl had covered every inch of the sheet with white paint. This episode of playful self-eradication occurred in a school which had never been segregated. It illustrates the extent to which cleanliness control and loss of social self-esteem may become associated in childhood. But it also points to the depth of the identity disturbance caused in people who are made to feel so inexorably "different" that legal desegregation can only be the beginning of a long and painful inner re-identification—not to speak of true participation in a more inclusive new identity.

The self-images cultivated during *all the childhood stages* thus gradually prepare the sense of identity, beginning with that earliest mutual recognition of and by another face which

the ethologists have made us look for in our human beginnings. Their findings, properly transposed into the human condition, may throw new light on the identity-giving power of
the eyes and the face which first "recognize" you (give you
your first "*Ansehen*"), and new light also on the infantile origin of the dreaded estrangement, the "loss of face." To be a
person, identical with oneself, presupposes a basic trust in one's
origins—and the courage to emerge from them.

I review these matters here, because every deeply upsetting
or uprooting experience brings about a partial regression both
to the basic hope for recognition and the basic horror of its
failure: the dead, the still-born identity. It is for this reason
that uprooted people often seem hardly to hear what you say,
but "hang on" to your eyes and your tone of voice.

But while a deep identity confusion in adolescence always
leads back to the infantile beginnings of "recognition," unsolved identity problems—as the case of the Wandering Jew
illustrated—can reach into old age where they may become
part of that despair which begrudges to the old person his own
recognition of the worthwhileness of his life. A man who is
hindered from living out his life is thereby deprived of the
right to *die actively*, as the agent of a living cause. René Spitz's
pictorial descriptions of infants who had no meaningful beginning [7] could be complemented by an impressive gallery depicting the lifeless faces of those who do not expect a meaningful end. But this does not suggest that aging man should be
encouraged forever to seek readjustments of his identity. Far
from it. Where identity formation is relatively successful in
youth, psychosocial development leads through the fulfillment
of adult phases to a final integrity, the possession of a few principles which though gleaned from changing experience yet
prove unchangeable in essence. Without old people in possession of such integrity, young people in need of an identity can
neither rebel nor obey.

The key problem of identity, then, is (as the term connotes) the capacity of the ego to sustain sameness and continuity in the face of changing fate. But fate always combines changes in inner conditions, which are the result of ongoing life stages, and changes in the milieu, the historical situation. Identity connotes the resiliency of maintaining essential patterns in the processes of change. Thus, strange as it may seem, it takes a well-established identity to tolerate radical change, for the well-established identity has arranged itself around basic values which cultures have in common. We may think here of the Polish peasant's values of family, work, and religion, which could be transferred relatively intact to the city blocks and steel mills of Pittsburgh, from the mud and fertility of the Polish prairie to the smog and the productivity of modern industry. Or we may think of the "primitive" and isolated Yemenites' adherence to *The Book* as a link over the centuries with the modern world of literacy; and of Ben-David's general observation that those immigrants have a better chance of becoming absorbed into Israeli society who bring with them a well-integrated self-image and group identity. These examples also indicate that identity does not connote a closed inner system impervious to change, but rather a psychosocial process which preserves some essential features in the individual as well as his society.

The danger of any period of large-scale uprooting and transmigration is that exterior crises will, in too many individuals and generations, upset the hierarchy of developmental crises and their built-in correctives; and that man will lose those roots that must be planted firmly in meaningful life cycles. For man's true roots are nourished in the sequence of generations and he loses his taproots in disrupted developmental time, not in abandoned localities. This is the real damage done by large-scale enforced migration—a damage which creeps into the process of generations and becomes a terrifying counterpart to the new threat of hereditary damage from nuclear explosions.

WHETHER, as clinicians or administrators, we are charged with the cure, the transit, or the rehabilitation of others, we become the guardians of lost life stages: ideally speaking, our work of rehabilitation should at least provide a meaningful *moratorium*, a period of delay in further commitment. As you well know, there can be in the very act of taking refuge an initial momentum of faith, of increased energy, and of the readiness for meaningful hardship, all of which disintegrates only in the second stage, the processing. This again is a common problem encountered by social and psychiatric workers. Let me briefly discuss the problem of the hospitalized patient: the parallels, I hope, will be obvious.

Hospitalized patients, having been committed, are often ready to commit themselves. They expect "to go to work," both on themselves and on whatever task they may be asked to do. But too often they are met by a laborious process of diagnosis and initiation which emphasizes the absolute distance of patienthood from active life. Thus literally "insult is added to injury" in that the uprooted one, already considered expendable or abnormal by his previous group of affiliation, finds himself categorized and judged by those who were expected to show him the way through a meaningful moratorium. Many a man acquires the irreversible identity of being a lifelong patient and client not on the basis of what he "is," but on the basis of what is first done about him.

The problem of the lost momentum of initial commitment, of course, only aggravates another danger intrinsic to prolonged uprootedness and institutionalization. I refer to the formation of *negative identities*, that is, of debased self-images and social roles. I have already indicated the difference in popular evaluation between the pioneer and the refugee, the frontiersman and the migrant. Add to this the traditional images of the "gypsies," the "shiftless," and the "vagrants" on the one hand, and of the "inmates," and the "interned" on the other, and you have a formidable array of negative evaluations which men in uprooted or confined conditions must contend with, either by resisting them to the last, or by accepting them. Prolonged passivity brings such marginal identities to the fore, makes them central and dominant in a formidable rearrangement of self-images not eradicable for generations. Informed therapeutic management, however, recognizes them as that secondary social disease which adheres to all enforced idleness and institutional patienthood.

Let me speak for a moment of the Austen Riggs Center, an open psychiatric hospital and a research foundation of which I am a staff member. We experience surprising examples of initiative among our patients wherever and whenever we ourselves can overcome certain diagnostic and prognostic prejudices by which we tend to overprotect them and simplify our task "for their own good." As much under the patients' pressure as the staff's we have initiated a "common work" program, which unites the patients in the morning for some hospital maintenance work. Thus patients of means can make an indirect contribution to the support of those in need of "scholarships." Before this plan worked, we would not have judged it feasible. In addition, a more individualized "activities program" was designed by Joan Erikson with the help of staff and patient committees. In the frame of this program and under the guidance of a professional teacher, our patients run a nursery school open to the children of the town. Before parents brought their children, and brought them again, we would not have thought this possible. Our activities program also includes a drama group, supervised by a professional director. Let me tell you of an instructive experience. On one occasion a group of young men patients decided to put on a difficult play under the direction of one of them. They entered their production in a yearly contest in a neighboring city where they competed with amateur theater groups from larger cities and from academic drama departments. The "Riggs Drama Group" won first prize. After the awards ceremony, some other contestants took me aside and asked for a clarification. The young players, they said, had done superbly, but they seemed hardly old enough *to be doctors* . . .

I need not underscore the significance of situations in which the patient can secure true communal recognition for a craftsmanlike job. This is especially important for young patients, in whom the process of identity formation at its most acute should not be linked with a negative self-image, even though (or just because) young people play and experiment with the idea of being outsiders, delinquents, rebels and patients. Some of our young patients, often the children of men of unlimited means or unsurpassable accomplishments, sport the costume of vagrants. But, as you know, in thus rebelling they are, in fact, conforming to a world-wide movement of youths loudly displaying "negative identities" and mocking with their eccentric dress an older generation, which over-typed its children and prejudged their identities.

Both patienthood by exterior uprooting, and the condition of psychiatric patienthood thus verge on the area of *active self-uprooting*. This can characterize shiftless but also truly adventurous individuals as well as spiritually restless and, on occasion, really creative ones: the agents of rejuvenation. To those, however, who act and sport the position of "outsider" for its own sake I would recommend the insight of Albert Camus, who created our time's supreme literary expression for man's existential status as *l'étranger*, and yet who gives due credit to the great importance in his younger years of the logic and the ethics—of soccer football. To fathom the limits of human existence you must have fully experienced, at some concrete time and space, the "rules of the game." To live as a philosophical "stranger" is one of the choices of mature man; to have that choice the immature person must, with our help, first find a home in the actuality of work and love.

It was Camus who reminded our youth of "that part of man that must always be defended." And youth—insofar as it is not bound to militant ideologies—attempts to defend that essence in many paradoxical and contradictory ways: by overacting or doing nothing, by rejecting all introspection or by overdoing it. It is not always clear, and yet often true, that the young thus refuse to offer their loyalty to outworn moralities in order to be loyal to some dimly divined ethics. In our country, some of our intellectual youth falls prey to a mixture of European existentialism and Eastern philosophy which seems to provide a late ideological rationale for some homegrown individualism. It cares little about the way in which mysticism or monasticism, in ongoing cultures, was rooted in the temporal concerns and the systematic moralities of their times and places. Yet, at any time of history, in order to lose one's identity, one must first have one; and in order to transcend, one must pass through and not bypass ethical concerns. Meditative monasticism, at its height, payed full recognition to all creation; and it took care of what existed by charitable work, by taking charge of the avenues of transcendence, and by accepting the responsibility for not generating what it could not or did not wish to take care of. Compared with this ethical position, I find our literary salesmen of partial conversion and of part-time mysticism obsessed by rather than freed from their selves. For he who is really aware of "that part of man that must always be defended" surely must accept responsibility for not denying that part, by action or by default, to those with whom he shares and in whom he augments human existence. Should they not, also, be given a chance to reach their "ultimate concern" unmarred by neurotic rootlessness?

IN CONCLUSION, let me discuss our use of arboreal terms in this matter of man's "roots": the imagery of man as a being grounded in a locality, supported by roots and absorbing organic nourishment from an ecologically bound universe. Has man always spoken of a loss of roots? Other eras have known large and disastrous migrations, and the man of the late Middle Ages must have felt his world as unrecognizably changed by the printing press and gunpowder, by the plague, and by the conquest of the seven seas, as we, in a larger world, find our world expanded and yet sharply contracted by radio communication and the nuclear bomb, by mental unrest, and the conquest of outer space. Is not the nostalgic emphasis on roots a reaction to the willful and creative transcendence of a primarily agricultural and "home town" existence at the beginning of the modern era? As long as man can fit his own life cycle entirely into the natural cycles of a segment of nature which he has learned to exploit, he can maintain a sense of participation—call it parasitic or symbiotic—in the roots which he cultivates. The resulting imagery of rootedness and growth has supported (as does all integrated imagery) some simple dignity and beauty, but it has also fostered special forms of rigidity and depravity which are subsequently ignored by the romantic seekers after a "return to roots." We find such seeking in our own ranks, where a preference for images of personal "growth" and of a rootedness of the individual in himself marks a reaction to the seemingly more "mechanistic" concepts of psychoanalysis. But whether we use images of the laboratory, the factory or the arboretum we must beware lest the mere sound of our terms makes us believe that we have gained more relevant concepts for human development.

Let me summarize those inner estrangements which are intrinsic to man's ontogenesis as an individual—so intrinsic, in fact, that adult conditions of uprootedness, of abandonment, and of isolation only echo what he already knows "from way back." I would suggest that this reverberation of the individual past in every historical disaster can induce man to submit to unjust suffering, and to accept persecution as part of "the human condition." But this also means that we will not erase in-

justice and persecution until we understand man's inner proclivity to persecute himself and thus to identify himself with
his persecutor.

The over-all fact is that man is apt to feel uprooted within
himself on every step of his development as a distinctive person. It begins early, for hardly has he learned to recognize the
familiar face (the original harbor of basic trust) when he becomes also frightfully aware of the unfamiliar, the strange face,
the unresponsive, the averted, the darkened, and the frowning
face (the "*fremdelt*," in German). And here begins, as psychoanalysis suggests, that inexplicable tendency on man's part
to feel that he has caused the face to turn away which happened to turn elsewhere.

Some other species, too, experience moments of intense recognition, such as are so flamboyantly displayed in the cere-
monies and dances of some birds which establish or re-estab-
lish the familiarity of species or of biological parentage. But
in man, all this becomes part of a highly individualized meeting of eyes, of faces, and of minds. As this marks the beginning
of all individuality, it also remains the ultimate goal of man's
wishes: "but then shall I know even also as I am known." Along
the stony road, however, are the many moments when man
feels that he neither knows nor is known, neither has a face
nor recognizes one: his first uprootedness, regularly re-experi-
enced in migration—and in psychosis.

Later in childhood comes the time when the child enjoys
his autonomy, standing on his own feet, wobbly but his own.
He becomes aware of a whole circle of approving eyes which
make the space he masters both safe and secure. He learns to
suppress some of his willfulness for the reward of feeling at
one with the will of those around him. But, alas, the moments
of disapproval and shaming also come, when he is frowned
upon and laughed at, and blushes in anger not knowing with
whom he is most angry: his exposed self or the hostile watch-
ers. This, then, is the second uprootedness, that awareness of

an exposed self by which man becomes an outsider to himself. From here on he is never fully himself and never fully "them." He will try, at times, to become totally himself by identifying with his rebellious impulses; or try to become totally the others by making their laws his compulsions; or he may do both, with the result that he doubts himself as well as the others.

Still later, the development of a conscience can provide a sense of definition and of clarity, and can guide growing initiative in approved and fruitful directions. But it also brings the "bad conscience," "*das schlechte Gewissen*," a term which leaves curiously open whether it is a consciousness of badness, or a bad consciousness. At any rate, it is part of that "super-ego formation," which makes man his own inner, and worse, his often unconscious judge. The resulting inhibitions and repressions could be expressed in terms of alienation, for they can turn man's most intimate wishes and memories into alien territory.

These, then, are some of the inescapable inner divisions which come about as man, freed of his biological navel cord, finds his place in the social and moral universe. Much of what we ascribe to neurotic *anxiety* and much of what we ascribe to existential *dread* is really only man's distinctive form of *fear:* for as an animal, for the sake of survival, scans near and far with specialized senses fit for a special environment, man must scan both his inner and his outer environment for indications of permissible activity and for promises of identity.

Is he more "at home" in some environments and less in others? Romantic yearning and superficial travel make us overestimate the inner security as well as the outer safety of past times or of foreign conditions. But it certainly seems as though man has always been estranged both from nature and from his inner world, and that he has always attempted and periodically succeeded in making his impossible predicament livable and productive. There is no reason to insist that a technological world, as such, need weaken inner resources of adaptation which may, in fact, be replenished by the good will and the ingenuity of a communicating species.

Was *predatory* man not alienated? In Northern California I have seen Yurok Indians pray to their salmon. Tearfully they assured their prey that they meant no harm to his essence, that they were eating only that fleshy part of him that he could well afford to lose, and that they would let his scales return down-river and out into the ocean where they came from, so that from them new salmon could grow—and continue to come into the Yurok's nets. This is, of course, a perfect magic "fit" with a deep secret of nature, namely, the propagation of salmon. But the tone of voice and the content of the prayers leave no doubt that man, in such a predicament, combines images of the ontogenetic estrangement from the parental provider and the tribe's fear of losing an alien provision into one prayerful attitude. Take *agricultural* man: certainly the peasant's tortured superstitions should convince us that nature figures in his imagination not only as a benevolent mother and familiar abode, but also as a fickle enemy to be coerced with bitterly hard work and to be appeased with cunning rituals. The inner dangers of the *mercantile* world are by now familiar to us. He who sells and buys, loans and collects, soon will make competitors, commodities, and slaves out of all men—and out of himself, his women, and his children. To that extent, he will become inhuman and will lose all capacity for empathy. Finally, we come to *industrialization* where man turns other men and himself into tools and the machines he runs into machinery which runs him. Here, obviously, man reaches the impasse of his existence as a species, for he learns to perfect and to be blindly proud of the machinery of self-extermination.

Now, somewhere between the exploitation of nature and the self-exploitation of mercantile and mechanized man a gigantic transformation has taken place which first was the subject of Marx's passionate attention: it is the creation of middlemen between man and nature. And it dawns on us that the

technological world of today is about to create kinds of alienations too strange to be imagined. All this, however, must not
becloud the universality of the problem of technical estrangement which started with the creation of tools and the
development of a self-conscious brain at the beginning of
mankind. Nor should we overlook the fact that workers of the
mind, who are apt to distantiate their own awareness and
"humanness" from what they call the alienated blindness of
the mechanized masses, at times only indulge in self-deception.
For the work of the mind has its intrinsic technical alienation,
too, employing as it does methods which must cause guilt, even
where the pursuits seem otherworldly and peaceful: methods
of analyzing existence into verbal bits, of abstracting experience into concepts, of forcing reality into experiments, and
of taking—by calling them alienated—magic revenge on those
who un-selfconsciously wield the power of the existing technology. No wonder that the worker of the mind senses alienation all about him. The question is only, to what extent he, in
addition, learns to become a responsible balance to the temporal
forces which he studies, exploits, and deplores.

The search for roots, then, has taken on ever-new forms in
the mercantile and industrial eras. Mercantile man's eagerness
to ascribe to the fluctuations of the market a lawfulness analogous to the cycles of nature helped create a mercantile kind of
genius but left many men with a sense of victimization in the
face of inhuman and ungodly chance. Industrial man's attempt
to identify with the machine as if it were a new totem animal
leads him into a self-perpetuating race for robot-like efficiency,
and yet also to the question as to what, when all adjustments
are made, is left of a human "identity." To worry about the
unchanging roots of human identity, then, may be as intrinsic
to an age of ruthless change as a widespread sense of guilt was
to the agricultural age, the technology of violated nature.

Guilt and fear for one's identity belong, of course, to the
built-in human equipment. Yet, particular forms of epidemic

apprehension seem to be period bound. And so it comes about that in this era of fantastically expanded mobility we are pre-occupied with roots and beginnings and first elements—and, incidentally, with the relationship between mother and child, as if in psychology, too, we must keep tracing development back to the psychic and the somatic navel cord. And, indeed, we may thus make renewed contact with the ontogenetic source of hope, with woman's most basic role in man's universe, and with the roots of an ethics which may yet—because it must—surpass man's proud inventions.

As WE LOOK AROUND we see that the man of today (and not only his American prototype) enjoys his automotive powers to the point of locomotive self-intoxication—and with a new kind of autocratic ruthlessness. If we are to tell this man that his mental health calls for roots, we will have to specify that minimum of root which he will need while in motion and that maximum which he can take along—much as the laboratories are expected to show him the limits of his intrusion into outer space and of his surrender to velocities which were not god-mothers at his birth. His discomfort over being all too rootless is rather well expressed in the joke about the man who boasted that he had paid five thousand dollars for his new electric auto-mobile. In view of the smallness of the car, his friends wondered about the price. "Oh," he said, "the car itself only cost a thousand dollars, but the extension cord cost four thousand."

The sense of rootlessness, in turn, has contributed much to what is discussed so widely as the alienation of technological man. But man's relation to nature, whether he trapped and slaughtered wildlife or bent plant life and animals to cultivation and domestication, was always a most complex one; because together with the capacity to invent tools goes that inner split of conscience which must do for man in his cultured and invented world what instinct does for the animal in its ecology. As psychoanalysis has verified, this process has created in man a sense of being uprooted from his own animal nature, and of being abandoned or expelled by his own conscience. In his fear and his guilt he tends to "make like" a tree, or an animal, or a machine. And, indeed, why should not man, a loco-motor being, equipped with an inventive brain as well as a sensitive conscience, create a mechanical world reasonably well fitted to his striving for a cultural and technological identity? Why should he not be at home (as much as it is his lot to be at home in any technology) managing whatever energies he can extract from nature to create whatever synthetic products he can fuse into a new style? For his identity as a tool-using creature is always the condition (if only the condition) of his spiritual search of a transcendent identity.

At any rate, as representatives of the professions concerned with mental health we are giving our active approval to mechanization through our very use of the streamlined machines which bring us together from so many countries, and of the communication equipment which permits us to listen to each other in many languages at once. Our professional struggle is with the magic thinking, the social exploitation, and the thoughtless destructiveness which always have a hand in man's mastery of tools and weapons. We challenge *man-made patient-hoods*, regardless of the exalted theories or ideologies which mask them as inevitabilities. We insist on the principle that no man should be robbed of the fruits of a lifetime, which alone permit him to face up to the central tasks of his existence in his era.

IV

Human Strength and
the Cycle of Generations

With the fourth lecture the focus shifts from the inner and outer hazards of ego development to those basic human strengths which have evolved with man's prolonged childhood and with his institutions and traditions. This lecture is an expansion of an address given for the Psychoanalytic Institute and the Mt. Zion Medical Center in San Francisco, in 1960, in memory of Sophie Mirviss, M.D.

1. A SCHEDULE OF VIRTUES

THE PSYCHOANALYST has good reason to show restraint in speaking about human virtue. For in doing so lightly he could be suspected of ignoring the evidential burden of his daily observations which acquaints him with the "much furrowed ground from which our virtues proudly spring." And he may be accused of abandoning the direction of Freudian thought in which conscious values can find a responsible re-evaluation only when the appreciation of the unconscious and of the irrational forces in man is firmly established.

Yet the very development of psychoanalytic thought, and its present preoccupation with "ego strength," suggests that human strength be reconsidered, not in the sense of nobility and rectitude as cultivated by moralities, but in the sense of "inherent strength." For I believe that psychoanalysts, in listening to life-histories for more than half a century, have developed an "unofficial" image of the strengths inherent in the individual life cycle and in the sequence of generations. I think here of those most enjoyable occasions when we can agree that a patient has really improved—not, as the questionnaires try to make us say, markedly improved, or partially improved —but essentially so. Here, the loss of symptoms is mentioned only in passing, while the decisive criterion is an increase in the strength and staying power of the patient's concentration on pursuits which are somehow right, whether it is in love or in work, in home life, friendship, or citizenship. Yet, we truly shy away from any systematic discussion of human strength. We recognize, for example, an inner affinity between the earliest and deepest mental disturbances and a radical loss of a basic kind of hope; or between the relation of compulsive and impulsive symptoms and a basic weakness in will. Yet, we are not curious to know what the genetic or dynamic determinants of a state of hope or of a state of controlled will power really are. In fact, we do our tortured best to express what we value in terms of double negatives; a person whom we would declare reasonably well is relatively resistant to regression, or somewhat freer from repression, or less given to ambivalence than might be expected. And yet we know that in a state of health or of mental and affective clarity a process of order takes over which is not and cannot be subsumed under the most complete list of negatives. Some of this process we call "ego-synthesis," and we gradually accumulate new observations under this heading. But we know that this process too, in some men in some moments and on some occasions, is endowed with a total quality which we might term "animated" or "spirited." This I certainly will not try to classify. But I will submit that, without acknowledging its existence, we cannot maintain any true perspective regarding the best moments of man's balance—nor the deepest of his tragedy.

In what follows I intend to investigate, then, first the developmental roots and later the evolutionary rationale of certain basic human qualities which I will call virtues. I do so, partially because I find the plural "strengths" awkward, but most of all because the word virtue serves to make a point. In

Latin virtue meant virility, which at least suggests the combination of *strength*, *restraint* and *courage* to be conveyed here, although we would, of course, hesitate to consider manliness the official virtue of the universe, especially since it dawns on us that womanhood may be forced to bear the larger share in saving humanity from man's climactic and catastrophic aspirations. But old English gave a special meaning to the word "virtue" which does admirably. It meant *inherent strength* or *active quality*, and was used, for example, for the undiminished potency of well preserved medicines and liquors. Virtue and spirit once had interchangeable meanings—and not only in the virtue that endowed liquid spirits. Our question, then, is: what "virtue goes out" of a human being when he loses the strength we have in mind, and "by virtue of" what strength does man acquire that animated or spirited quality without which his moralities become mere moralism and his ethics feeble goodness?

I will call "virtue," then, certain human qualities of strength, and I will relate them to that process by which ego strength may be developed from stage to stage and imparted from generation to generation.

A SEEMING PARADOX of human life is man's collective power to create his own environment, although each individual is born with a naked vulnerability extending into a prolonged infantile dependence. The weakness of the newborn, however, is truly relative. While far removed from any measure of mastery over the physical world, newborn man is endowed with an appearance and with responses which appeal to the tending adults' tenderness and make them wish to attend to his needs; which arouse concern in those who are concerned with his well-being; and which, in making adults care, stimulate their active care-taking. I employ the repetition of the words tending, concern, and caring, not for poetic effect, but in order to underscore the fundamental fact that, in life in general and in human life in particular, the vulnerability of being newly born and the meekness of innocent needfulness have a power all their own. Defenseless as babies are, they have mothers at their command, families to protect the mothers, societies to support the structure of families, and traditions to give a cultural continuity to systems of tending and training. All of this, however, is necessary for the human infant to evolve humanly, for his environment must provide that outer wholeness and continuity which, like a second womb, permits the child to develop his separate capacities in distinct steps, and to unify them in a series of psychosocial crises.

In recent years, psychiatry has concerned itself with the mother-child relationship, and has at times burdened it with the whole responsibility for man's sanity and maturation. This concentration on earliest development seemed to find powerful support in the young science of ethology, which analyzes the innate mechanism by which mother animal and young animal release in each other the behavior necessary for the survival of the young—and thus the species. However, a true ethological comparison must juxtapose the first period in animal life (such as the nest-occupancy of certain birds) with man's whole pre-adult life, including adolescence. For man's psychosocial survival is safeguarded only by vital virtues which develop in the interplay of successive and overlapping generations, living together in organized settings. Here, living together means more than incidental proximity. It means that the individual's life-stages are "interliving," cogwheeling with the stages of others which move him along as he moves them. I have, therefore, in recent years, attempted to delineate the whole life-cycle as an integrated psychosocial phenomenon, instead of following what (in analogy to teleology) may be called the "originological" approach, that is, the attempt to derive the meaning of development primarily from a reconstruction of the infant's beginnings.

When it comes to naming the basic virtues, with which human beings steer themselves and others through life, one is at first tempted to make up new words out of Latin roots. Latin always suggests expertness and explicitness, while everyday words have countless connotations. To optimists they make virtues sound like gay and easy accomplishments, and to pessimists, like idealistic pretences. Yet when we approach phenomena closer to the ego, the everyday words of living languages, ripened in the usage of generations, will serve best as a basis of discourse.

I will, therefore, speak of *Hope, Will, Purpose,* and *Competence* as the rudiments of virtue developed in childhood; of *Fidelity* as the adolescent virtue; and of *Love, Care,* and *Wisdom* as the central virtues of adulthood. In all their seeming discontinuity, these qualities depend on each other. Will cannot be trained until hope is secure, nor can love become reciprocal until fidelity has proven reliable. Also, each virtue and its place in the schedule of all virtues is vitally interrelated to other segments of human development, such as the stages of psychosexuality which are so thoroughly explored in the whole of psychoanalytic literature,[1] the psychosocial crises,[2] and the steps of cognitive maturation.[3] These schedules I must take for granted, as I restrict myself to a parallel timetable of the evolving virtues.

IF WE ASCRIBE TO the healthy infant the rudiments of *Hope,* it would, indeed, be hard to specify the criteria for this state, and harder to measure it: yet he who has seen a hopeless child, knows what is *not* there. Hope is both the earliest and the most indispensable virtue inherent in the state of being alive. Others have called this deepest quality *confidence,* and I have referred to *trust* as the earliest positive psychosocial attitude, but if life is to be sustained hope must remain, even where confidence is wounded, trust impaired. Clinicians know that an adult who has lost all hope, regresses into as lifeless a state as a living organism can sustain. But there is something in the anatomy even of mature hope which suggests that it is the most childlike of all ego-qualities, and the most dependent for its verification on the charity of fate; thus religious sentiment induces adults to restore their hopefulness in periodic petitionary prayer, assuming a measure of childlikeness toward unseen, omnipotent powers.

Nothing in human life, however, is secured in its origin unless it is verified in the intimate meeting of partners in favorable social settings. The infant's smile inspires hope in the adult and, in making him smile, makes him wish to give hope; but this is, of course, only one physiognomic detail which indicates that the infant by his trustful search for experience and assurance, awakens in the giver a strength which he, in turn, is ready and needful to have awakened and to have consolidated by the experience of mutuality.

Hope relies for its beginnings on the new being's first encounter with *trustworthy maternal persons*, who respond to his need for *intake* and *contact* with warm and calming envelopment and provide food both pleasurable to ingest and easy to digest, and who prevent experience of the kind which may regularly bring too little too late. This is far from being a merely instinctive, or a merely instinctual matter. Biological motherhood needs at least three links with social experience: the mother's past experience of being mothered; a conception of motherhood shared with trustworthy contemporary surroundings; and an all-enveloping world-image tying past, present, and future into a convincing pattern of providence. Only thus can mothers provide.

Hope is verified by a combination of experiences in the individual's "prehistoric" era, the time before speech and verbal memory. Both psychoanalysis and genetic psychology consider central in that period of growth the secure apperception of an "object." The psychologists mean by this the ability to perceive the *enduring quality* of the *thing world* while psychoanalysts speak loosely of a first love-object, i.e., the experience of the care-taking person as a *coherent being*, who reciprocates one's physical and emotional needs in expectable ways and therefore deserves to be endowed with trust, and whose face is recognized as it recognizes. These two kinds of object are the first knowledge, the first verification, and thus the basis of hope.

Hope, once established as a basic quality of experience, remains independent of the verifiability of "hopes," for it is in the nature of man's maturation that concrete hopes will, at a time when a hoped-for event or state comes to pass, prove to have been quietly superseded by a more advanced set of hopes. The gradual widening of the infant's horizon of active experience provides, at each step, verifications so rewarding that they inspire new hopefulness. At the same time, the infant develops a greater capacity for renunciation, together with the ability to transfer disappointed hopes to better prospects; and he learns to dream what is imaginable and to train his expectations on what promises to prove possible. All in all, then, maturing hope not only maintains itself in the face of changed facts—it proves itself able to change facts, even as faith is said to move mountains. From an evolutionary point of view, it seems that hope must help man to approximate a measure of that rootedness possessed by the animal world, in which instinctive equipment and environment, beginning with the maternal response, verify each other, unless catastrophe overtakes the individual or the species. To the human infant, his mother *is* nature. She must *be* that original verification, which, later, will come from other and wider segments of reality. All the self-verifications, therefore, begin in that inner light of the mother-child-world, which Madonna images have conveyed as so exclusive and so secure: and, indeed, such light must continue to shine through the chaos of many crises, maturational and accidental.

To CHANCE SOME first formulations: *Hope is the enduring belief in the attainability of fervent wishes, in spite of the dark urges and rages which mark the beginning of existence.* Hope is the ontogenetic basis of faith, and is nourished by the adult faith which pervades patterns of care.

An exclusive condition of hopefulness, translated into various imaginable worlds, would be a paradise in nature, a Utopia in social reality, and a heaven in the beyond. In the individual, here and now, it would mean a maladaptive optimism. For true hope leads inexorably into conflicts between the rapidly developing self-will and the will of others from which the rudiments of will must emerge. As the infant's senses and his muscles grasp at opportunities for more active experience, he faces the double demand for self-control and for the acceptance of control from others. *To will* does not mean to be willful, but rather to gain gradually the power of increased judgment and decision in the application of drive. Man must learn to will what can be, to renounce as not worth willing what cannot be, and to believe he willed what is inevitable.

Here, no doubt, is the genetic origin of the elusive question of Free Will, which man, ever again, attempts to master logically and theologically. The fact is that no person can live, no ego remain intact without hope and will. Even philosophical man who feels motivated to challenge the very ground he stands on, questioning both will and hope as illusory, feels more real for having willed such heroic enquiry; and where man chooses to surrender his sense of having willed the inevitable to gods and leaders, he fervently endows them with what he has renounced for himself.

The rudiments of will are acquired, in analogy to all basic qualities, as the ego unifies experiences on fronts seemingly remote from one another: awareness and attention, manipulation, verbalization, and locomotion. The training of the eliminative sphincters can become the center of the struggle over inner and outer control which resides in the whole muscle system and its double executive: individual co-ordination and social guidance. A sense of defeat (from too little or too much training) can lead to deep *shame* and a compulsive *doubt* whether one ever really willed what one did, or really did what one willed.

If will, however, is built securely into the early development of the ego it survives, as hope does, the evidences of its limited potency, for the maturing individual gradually incorporates a knowledge of what is expectable and what can be expected of him. Often defeated, he nevertheless learns to accept the existential paradox of making decisions which he knows "deep down" will be predetermined by events, because making decisions is part of the evaluative quality inherent in being alive. Ego strength depends, above all, on the sense of having done one's active part in the chain of the inevitable. And as it is with lesser hopes, so it is with small wills (if the word is permitted). They do not really seem worth despairing over when the moment of testing arrives, provided only that growth and development have enough leeway to present new issues, and that, all in all, expectable reality proves more satisfactory and more interesting than fantasy.

Will, therefore, is the unbroken determination to exercise free choice as well as self-restraint, in spite of the unavoidable experience of shame and doubt in infancy. Will is the basis for the acceptance of law and necessity, and it is rooted in the judiciousness of parents guided by the spirit of law.

The social problem of will is contained in the words "good will." The good will of others obviously depends on a mutual limitation of wills. It is during the second and third year that the child must yield to newcomers. It is now the task of judicious parenthood to honor the privileges of the strong and yet protect the rights of the weak. It will gradually grant a measure of self-control to the child who learns to control willfulness, to offer willingness, and to exchange good will. But in the end the self-image of the child will prove to have been split in the way in which man is apt to remain split for the rest of his life. For even as the ideal ("pre-ambivalent," as we say) image of the loving mother brought with it the child's self-image as reflecting that mother's true recognition of the child as hers and as good, so does the ambivalently loved image of the controlling parent correspond to an ambivalently loved self, or rather selves. From here on, the able and the impotent, the loving and the angry, the unified and the self-contradictory selves will be part of man's equipment: truly a psychic fall from grace. In view of this inner split, only judicious parenthood, feeling itself part of a reasonably just civic and world order, can convey a healing sense of justice.

We now come to the third vital virtue: *Purpose*. And taking the principles of presentation for granted, we can now be briefer.

It is inherent in infantile man's prolonged immaturity that he must train the rudiments of will in situations in which he does not quite know what he wants and why, which makes his willfulness at times rather desperate. By the same token he must develop in "mere" fantasy and play the rudiments of purpose: a temporal perspective giving direction and focus to concerted striving. Play is to the child what thinking, planning, and blueprinting are to the adult, a trial universe in which conditions are simplified and methods exploratory, so that past failures can be thought through, expectations tested. The rules of play cannot be altogether imposed by the will of adults: toys and playmates are the child's equals. In the toy world, the child "plays out" the past, often in disguised form, in the manner of dreams, and he begins to master the future by anticipating it in countless variations of repetitive themes. In taking the various role-images of his elders into his sphere of make-believe, he can find out how it feels to be like them before fate forces him to become, indeed, like some of them. But if it seems that he spends on his play a sincere purposefulness out of proportion to what he soon must learn, namely, what things are "really for," what their "real purpose" is, we underestimate the evolutionary necessity for representational play in an animal who must learn to bind together an inner and an outer world, a remembered past and an anticipated future, before he can learn to master the tools used in co-operation, the roles distributed in a community, and the purposes pursued in a given technology.

Thus infantile play (like mature man's inspired toys: dance, drama, ritual) affords an intermediate reality in which purposefulness can disengage itself from fixations on the past. It seems significant that play is most intense when the period of infantile sexuality comes to an end and when that great human barrier, the universal "incest-taboo," is met. Sexual drive and purposeful energy must now be diverted from the very parental persons who first awakened the child's tenderness, sensuality, and amorphous sexual fantasies; and it is diverted toward a future first of fantastic but then more and more of realizable goals.

Play, in young animals, too, is predicated upon parental protection from hunger and from danger. In man it is, furthermore, dependent on protection from unmanageable conflict. The play age relies on the existence of the *family in one of its exemplary forms*, which must gradually delineate where play ends and irreversible purpose begins, where fantasy is no longer permissible and to-be-learned reality all-demanding: only thus is conscience integrated. It is not always understood that one of the main rationales for marital and familial loyalty is the imperative need for inner unity in the child's conscience at the very time when he can and must envisage goals beyond the family. For the voices and images of those adults who are now internalized as an *inner voice* must not contradict each other too flagrantly. They contribute to the child's most intense conscience development—a development which separates, once and for all, play and fantasy from that future which is irreversible. Threats, punishments, and warnings all have in common the designation of certain acts (and by implication, thoughts) as having a social and, indeed, eternal reality which can never be undone. Conscience accepts such irreversibility as internal and private, and it is all the more important that it incorporate the ethical example of a family purposefully united in familial and economic pursuits. This alone gives the child the inner freedom to move on—to whatever school setting his culture has ready for him.

Purposefulness is now ready to attach itself gradually to a sense of reality which is defined by what *can be attained* and by what can be *shared in words*. Thus, conscience, the consistent inner voice which delineates permissible action and thought, finds a powerful ally in the structure of language which verifies a shared actuality.

Purpose, then, is the courage to envisage and pursue valued goals uninhibited by the defeat of infantile fantasies, by guilt and by the foiling fear of punishment. It invests ideals of action and is derived from the example of the basic family. It is the strength of aim-direction fed by fantasy yet not fantastic, limited by guilt yet not inhibited, morally restrained yet ethically active. That man began as a playing child, however, leaves a residue of play-acting and role-playing even in what he considers his highest purposes. These he sees, as an adult, enacted in the tableaux of his past history; these he projects on a larger and more perfect future stage; and these he dramatizes in the ceremonial present with uniformed players in ritual arrangements.

WHAT SHALL WE CALL the next virtue? *Competence* comes closest to what I have in mind, although my friend, R. W. White, has reserved it for a principle active in all living.[4] Yet, it should not be too difficult to agree that a quality which endows all living should yet have its epigenetic crisis during one stage of the life cycle. A sense of competence, at any rate, characterizes what eventually becomes *workmanship*. Ever since his "expulsion from paradise," of course, man has been inclined to protest work as drudgery or as slavery, and to consider most fortunate those who seemingly can choose to work or not to work. The fact, however, is that man *must* learn to work, as soon as his intelligence and his capacities are ready to be "put to work," so that his ego's power may not atrophy.

Evolution has brought to pass that man, when he approaches the age of instruction in the basic elements of his culture's technology, is the most unspecialized of all animals. The rudiments of hope, will, and purpose anticipate a future of only dimly anticipated tasks. Now the child needs to be shown basic methods leading to the identity of a technical way of life. For (contrary to modern apostles of infantile Eros) infantile sexuality lacks any chance of competence, and if R. W. White would wish to oppose his theory of competence to the psychoanalytic theory of infantile sexuality, he could point out that in childhood the transitory investment of instinctual energy in erotic possibilities is intense, and often fateful, but that its dividends in satisfaction and completion are extremely limited. It makes sense, then, that a period of psychosexual latency should permit the human to develop the tool possibilities of body, mind, and thing-world and to postpone further progress along sexual and sensual lines until they become part of a larger area of social responsibility.

In school, what "works" in the fabric of one's thought and in the use of one's physical co-ordination can be found to "work" in materials and in co-operative encounters: a self-verification of lasting importance. All cultures, therefore, meet this stage with the offer of instruction in perfectible skills leading to practical uses and durable achievements. All cultures also have their logic and their "truths" which can be learned, by exercise, usage, and ritual. Where literacy is a common basis for future specialization, the rules of grammar and of algebra, of course, form a more abstract demonstration of the workings of reality. Thus the rudiments of competence and of reasonableness prepare in the child a future sense of workmanship without which there can be no "strong ego." Without it man feels inferior in his equipment, and in his ability to match an ever-increasing radius of manageable reality with his capacities.

The child at this stage, then, is ready for a variety of specializations and will learn most eagerly techniques in line with that *ethos of production* which has already entered his anticipations by way of ideal examples, real or mythical, and which now meets him in the persons of instructive adults and co-operative peers. It is thus that individual man develops at each stage a significant gain in human evolution by joining a larger section of his culture. In this case his developing capacities permit him to apprehend the basic materials of technology, and the elements of reasoning which make techniques teachable.

Competence, then, is the free exercise of dexterity and intelligence in the completion of tasks, unimpaired by infantile inferiority. It is the basis for co-operative participation in technologies and relies, in turn, on the logic of tools and skills.

WHEN MAN'S SEXUALITY MATURES in puberty, he is not yet ready to be a mate or a parent. There is, in fact, a real question whether early freedom in the direct use of his sexuality would make man freer as a person and as a guarantor of the freedom of others. At any rate, a youth's ego-balance is decidedly endangered by the double uncertainty of a newly matured sexual machinery which must be kept in abeyance in some or all of its functions while he prepares for his own place in the adult order. His consequent impulsiveness alternating with compulsive restraint is well-known and well-described. In all of this, however, an "ideological" seeking after an inner coherence and a durable set of values can always be detected; and I would call the particular ego-quality which emerges, with and from adolescence, *Fidelity*.[5]

Fidelity is the ability to sustain loyalties freely pledged in spite of the inevitable contradictions of value systems. It is the cornerstone of identity and receives inspiration from confirming ideologies and affirming companions.

In youth, such truth verifies itself in a number of ways: a high sense of duty, accuracy, and veracity in the rendering of reality; the sentiment of truthfulness, as in sincerity and conviction; the quality of genuineness, as in authenticity; the trait of loyalty, of "being true"; fairness to the rules of the game; and finally all that is implied in devotion—a freely given but binding vow, with the fateful implication of a curse befalling traitors. When Hamlet, the emotional victim of his royal parents' faithlessness, poses the question, "To be or not to be," he demonstrates in word and deed that to him "to be" is contingent on being loyal (to the self, to love, to the crown) and that the rest is death. Cultures, societies, religions offer the adolescent the nourishment of some truth in rites and rituals of confirmation as a member of a totem, a clan, or a faith, a nation or a class, which henceforth is to be his super-family; in modern times we also find powerful ideologies which claim and receive the loyalty (and, if demanded, an early death) from youth. For youth needs, above all, confirming adults and affirming peers. Identity owes its evolutionary and historical significance to the fact that, so far, social groups of men, no longer constituting a species in nature and not yet the mankind of history, have needed to feel with vanity or conviction that they were of some *special* kind, which promised to each individual the participation in a select identity.

Tribal, national, and class identity, however, demand that

man consider otherness inimical, and at least some men have overdefined others as enemies, treating them with an arbitrary ferocity absent from the animal world. At any rate, the need for superior status-identity combined with technological pride has made man exploit and annihilate other men with complete equanimity. Whatever level of technology man has reached he can regress to archaic pursuits with a vengeance: he can hunt down men of another race or nation or class; he can enslave them in masses; he can trade them out of property and liberty; he can butcher them in public "furors" or discreetly design their mass destruction. Perhaps even more astonishing, he can treat his own children as "others": as "soil" to be implanted with his values; as animals to be whipped and tamed; as property to be disposed of; and as cheap labor to be exploited. All this, at one time or another, has been a part of an ethos of a technology so self-righteous that even highminded men could not afford to act otherwise without seeming to be traitors to some superiority, or despoilers of some solidarity. In our era of limitless technological expansion, therefore, the question will be what man can afford and decide *not* to use, *not* to invent and *not* to exploit—and yet save his identity.

But here we enter the domain of ethical values. Identity and fidelity are necessary for ethical strength, but they do not provide it in themselves. It is for adult man to provide content for the ready loyalty of youth, and worthy objects for its need to repudiate. As cultures, through graded training, enter into the fiber of young individuals, they also absorb into their life-blood the rejuvenative power of youth. Adolescence is thus a vital regenerator in the process of social evolution; for youth selectively offers its loyalties and energies to the conservation of that which feels true to them and to the correction or destruction of that which has lost its regenerative significance.

Loyal and legal are kindred words. He who can be loyal can bind himself legally—or decide to remain deviant or become revolutionary in loyalty to an overdue rejuvenation. As the young adult selects those who in turn will select him—as members, friends, mates and co-workers—he completes the foundation for the adult virtues. His identity and his style of fidelity define his place in what history has determined as his environment; but so does his society define itself by the way it absorbs (or fails to absorb) his powers of solidarity.

In our day, ideologies take over where religion leaves off, presenting themselves (in addition to other, more practical claims) as historical perspectives on which to fasten individual faith and collective confidence. As religions do, they counteract a threatening sense of alienation with positive ritual and affirmative dogma, and with a rigorous and cruel ban on alienisms in their own ranks or in foreign enemies. They do not hesitate to combine magic with technique by amplifying the sound of One Voice speaking out of the night, and by magnifying and multiplying One Face in the spotlights of mass gatherings. Most relevant in the present connection, however, is the way in which ideologies tie dogmas to new scientific and technological developments. For it must be obvious that science and technology in our day provide a most immediate form of verification by the material riches available to all who are willing and able to work, and, above all, to help to make things work.

THAT *Love* IS THE GREATEST of human virtues, and, in fact, the dominant virtue of the universe, is so commonly assumed that it will be well to consider once more its evolutionary rationale, and to state why love is here assigned to a particular stage and a particular crisis in the unfolding human life cycle. Does not love bind together every stage? There are, to be sure, many forms of love, from the infant's comfortable and anxious attachment to his mother to the adolescent's passionate and desperate infatuation; but love in the evolutionary and generational sense is, I believe, the transformation of the love received throughout the preadolescent stage of life into the care given to others during adult life.

It must be an important evolutionary fact that man, over and above sexuality, develops a selectivity of love: I think it is the *mutuality of mates and partners in a shared identity*, for the mutual verification through an experience of finding oneself, as one loses oneself, in another. For let me emphasize here that identity proves itself strongest where it can take chances with itself. For this reason, love in its truest sense presupposes both identity and fidelity. While many forms of love can be shown to be at work in the formation of the various virtues, it is important to realize that only graduation from adolescence permits the development of that intimacy, the selflessness of joined devotion, which anchors love in a mutual commitment. Intimate love thus is the guardian of that elusive and yet all-pervasive power in psycho-social evolution: the power of *cultural and personal style*, which gives and demands conviction in the shared patterns of living, guarantees individual identity in joint intimacy, and binds into a "way of life" the affiliations of procreation and of production.

The love of young adulthood is, above all, a *chosen*, an *active* love, no matter what the methods of matrimonial selection are which make such a choice a pre-condition for familiarity or lead to it by a process of gradual familiarization. In either case, the problem is one of transferring the experience of being cared for in a parental setting, in which one happened to grow up, to a new, an adult affiliation which is actively chosen and cultivated as a mutual concern.

The word "affiliation" literally means to adopt somebody as a son—and, indeed, in friendships and partnerships young adults become sons of each other, but sons by a free choice which verifies a long hope for kinship beyond (incestuous) blood-bonds. From here on, ego-strength depends on an affiliation with others who are equally ready and able to share in the task of caring for offspring, products, and ideas.

Adult sexuality is marked by genitality, by the capacity for a full and mutual consummation of the sexual act. An immense power of verification pervades this meeting of bodies and temperaments after a hazardously long childhood, which, as the study of neuroses has revealed in detail, can severely prejudice the capacity for psychosexual mutuality. Freud observed that mature genitality alone guarantees that combination (by no means easily acquired, nor easily maintained) of intellectual clarity, sexual mutuality, and considerate love, which anchors man in the actuality of his responsibilities.

We have, so far, said nothing about the differences between the sexes, and for once, this neglect has a justification. For it is only in young adulthood that the biological differences between the sexes—and I believe that they are decisive from the beginning—pass their psychosocial crisis and result in a polarization of the two sexes within a joint life-style. The previously established virtues are preparatory to such polarization and to such style, as are all the physical powers and cognitive capacities developing up to and through adolescence. Competence as such is an intersexual virtue, and so is fidelity. One could make a point for an evolutionary rationale which would explain why sexual differences should not fully divide the sexes until competence and fidelity permit their division to be one of polarization, that is, one of mutual enhancement of experience and of distribution of labor within a stylized pattern of love and care. Such a rationale of human development would also suggest that the sexes are less different in regard to the capacities and virtues which further communication and cooperation; while the differences are greatest where divergence is of the essence, that is, in the counterpoints of love life and the divided functions of procreation.[6] One could say, then, that the sexes are most similar in the workings of the ego, which—being closest to consciousness, language and ethics—must serve both to integrate the fact of sexual mutuality and bipolarity.

Love, then, is mutuality of devotion forever subduing the antagonisms inherent in divided function. It pervades the intimacy of individuals and is thus the basis of ethical concern.

Yet, love can also be joint selfishness in the service of some territoriality, be it bed or home, village or country. That such "love," too, characterizes his affiliations and associations is at least one reason for man's clannish adherence to styles which he will defend "as if his life depended on them." His ego's coherence, his certainty of orientation, *do* depend on them; and it is for this reason that ego-panic can make man "go blind" with a rage which induces him, in the righteous defense of a shared identity, to sink to levels of sadism for which there seems to be no parallel in the animal world.

Care IS A QUALITY essential for psychosocial evolution, for we are the teaching species. Animals, too, instinctively encourage in their young what is ready for release, and, of course, some animals can be taught some tricks and services by man. Only man, however, can and must extend his solicitude over the long, parallel and overlapping childhoods of numerous offspring united in households and communities. As he transmits the rudiments of hope, will, purpose and competence, he imparts meaning to the child's bodily experiences, he conveys a logic much beyond the literal meaning of the words he teaches, and he gradually outlines a particular world image and style of fellowship. All of this is necessary to complete in man the analogy to the basic, ethological situation between parent animal and young animal. All this, and no less, makes us comparable to the ethologist's goose and gosling. Once we have grasped this interlocking of the human life stages, we understand that adult man is so constituted as to *need to be needed* lest he suffer the mental deformation of self-absorption, in which he becomes his own infant and pet. I have, therefore, postulated an instinctual and psychosocial stage of "generativity" beyond that of genitality. Parenthood is, for most, the first, and for many, the prime generative encounter [7] yet the perpetuation of mankind challenges the generative ingenuity of workers and thinkers of many kinds. And man *needs* to teach, not only for the sake of those who need to be taught, and not only for the fulfillment of his identity, but because facts are kept alive by being told, logic by being demonstrated, truth by being professed. Thus, the teaching passion is not restricted to the teaching profession. Every mature adult knows the satisfaction of explaining what is dear to him and of being understood by a groping mind.

Care is the widening concern for what has been generated by love, necessity, or accident; it overcomes the ambivalence adhering to irreversible obligation.

Generativity, as the instinctual power behind various forms of selfless "caring," potentially extends to whatever a man generates and leaves behind, creates and produces (or helps to produce). The ideological polarization of the Western world which has made Freud the century's theorist of sex, and Marx that of work, has, until quite recently, left a whole area of man's mind uncharted in psychoanalysis. I refer to man's *love for his works and ideas as well as for his children*, and the necessary self-verification which adult man's ego receives, and must receive, from his labor's challenge. As adult man needs to be needed, so—for the strength of his ego and for that of his community—he requires the challenge emanating from what he has generated and from what now must be "brought up," guarded, preserved—and eventually transcended.

Man's creation of all-caring gods is not only an expression of his persisting infantile need for being taken care of, but also a projection onto a super-human agency of an ego-ideal. This agency has to be strong enough to guide (or at least forgive) man's propensity for freely propagating offspring, causing events and creating conditions which, ever again, prove to be beyond him. It is obvious, however, that man must now learn to accept the responsibility which evolution and history have given him, and must learn to guide and planfully restrain his capacity for unlimited propagation, invention and expansion. And here I emphatically include woman, when I speak of man. For woman's preparation for care is anchored more decisively in her body, which is, as it were, the morphological model of care, at once protective abode and fountain of food.

Modern man, forced to limit his fertility, is apt to consider the matter of procreative involvement resolved by the technical possibility of making a conscious choice in the matter of fertilization. For such choice, men must be readied. Yet an ever so "safe" love life, if accompanied by a mere avoidance of offspring and a denial of generativity, could be, in some, as severe a source of inner tension as the denial of sexuality itself has been. There could well arise the specific guilt of playing with the "fire of creation." It is essential, therefore, that the control of procreation be guided not only by an acknowledgment of man's psychosexual needs, but also by a universal sense of generative responsibility toward all human beings brought planfully into this world. This would include (beyond contraceptives and food packages) the joint guarantee to each child of a chance for such development as we are outlining here.

As WE COME TO the last stage, we become aware of the fact that our civilization really does not harbor a concept of the whole of life, as do the civilizations of the East: "In office a Confucian, in retirement a Taoist." In fact, it is astonishing to behold, how (until quite recently and with a few notable exceptions) Western psychology has avoided looking at the range of the whole cycle.[8] As our world-image is a one-way street to never ending progress interrupted only by small and big catastrophes, our lives are to be one-way streets to success —and sudden oblivion. Yet, if we speak of a cycle of life we really mean two cycles in one: the cycle of one generation concluding itself in the next, and the cycle of individual life coming to a conclusion. If the cycle, in many ways, turns back on its own beginnings, so that the very old become again like children, the question is whether the return is to a childlikeness seasoned with wisdom—or to a finite childishness. This is not only important within the cycle of individual life, but also within that of generations, for it can only weaken the vital fiber of the younger generation if the evidence of daily living verifies man's prolonged last phase as a sanctioned period of childishness. Any span of the cycle lived without vigorous meaning, at the beginning, in the middle, or at the end, endangers the sense of life and the meaning of death in all whose life stages are intertwined.

Individuality here finds its ultimate test, namely, man's existence at the entrance to that valley which he must cross alone. I am not ready to discuss the psychology of "ultimate concern." But in concluding my outline, I cannot help feeling that the order depicted suggests an existential complementarity of the great Nothingness and the actuality of the cycle of generations. For if there is any responsibility in the cycle of life it must be that one generation owes to the next that strength by which it can come to face ultimate concerns in its own way—unmarred by debilitating poverty or by the neurotic concerns caused by emotional exploitation.

For each generation must find the wisdom of the ages in the form of its own wisdom. Strength in the old, therefore, takes the form of wisdom in all of its connotations from ripened "wits" to accumulated knowledge and matured judgment. It is the essence of knowledge freed from temporal relativity. *Wisdom, then, is detached concern with life itself, in the face of death itself*. It maintains and conveys the integrity of experience, in spite of the decline of bodily and mental functions. It responds to the need of the on-coming generation for an integrated heritage and yet remains aware of the relativity of all knowledge.

Potency, performance, and adaptability decline; but if vigor of mind combines with the gift of responsible renunciation, some old people can envisage human problems in their entirety (which is what "integrity" means) and can represent to the coming generation a living example of the "closure" of a style of life. Only such integrity can balance the despair of the knowledge that a limited life is coming to a conscious conclusion, only such wholeness can transcend the petty disgust of feeling finished and passed by, and the despair of facing the period of relative helplessness which marks the end as it marked the beginning.

There are the leaders, of course, and the thinkers, who round out long productive lives in positions in which wisdom is of the essence and is of service. There are those who feel verified in a numerous and vigorous progeny. But they, too, eventually join the over-aged who are reduced to a narrowing space-time, in which only a few things, in their self-contained form, offer a last but firm whisper of confirmation.

2. EVOLUTION AND EGO

As I reviewed with you an epigenetic schedule of emergent virtues, you were, no doubt, as concerned as I am over the probability that this ascending list will be eagerly accepted by some as a potential inventory for tests of adjustment, or as a new production schedule in the manufacture of desirable children, citizens, and workers. But all such attempts will be shortlived, because they will not work, not even on paper. Others may foresee the use of the schedule as a new set of ideals, to be held up with moral fervor: this by their very nature *these* virtues cannot be. But perhaps we should be more concerned about the list itself, as it stands, for my selection of virtues and their distribution throughout the cycle of life may well appear rather arbitrary. I remember here, with some discomfort, one of my favorite Viennese stories. An Austrian Emperor was asked to pass judgment on the model of a baroque statue which was to adorn one of Vienna's squares.

He studied it for a while with the concentration expected of a patron of the arts and then decreed with authority: "It needs some more faith-hope-and-charity down there on the left." Have I viewed the whole of life the way the Emperor judged the statue?

I hope to have indicated that these emergent virtues are not external ornaments easily added or omitted according to the fancies of esthetic or moral style. This whole "body" of virtues is, in fact, anchored in three different systems which I would like to remark on in some detail. They are: *epigenesis* in individual development; the *sequence of generations;* and the *growth of the ego.* Let me first approach epigenesis.

At a meeting in 1955, a number of workers in child development discussed the question of whether there were discernible "general stages" in childhood—stages clearly encompassing (*englobe*) the different functions of body and mind—which develop at the same time and yet seem to maintain such remarkable autonomy from each other.[9] Jean Piaget was one of the discussants and was, as usual, both sharply rigorous in the pursuit of known method, and amusing in his asides. He doubted the existence of such unified stages on physiological grounds, reiterating that, for example, the dental, skeletal, cerebral and endocrine systems grow and develop at their own rates. He took for granted that, in the healthy child, there is, at any given time, a high degree of *functional unity*, that is, an ability to reconcile and co-ordinate the growth patterns of all the physiological as well as the mental and emotional functions. This he called the *unity of personality*. But he discarded, as unproven, any claim of having found the principles governing this functional unity at a given stage in such a way that a *structural unity* for that particular stage could be demonstrated. Offering himself as an example of a personality "*multiple, divisée et contradictoire,*" he granted that on professional occasions he could force himself to be quite serious, while on other (unspecified) occasions, he had to consider himself rather childish or was apt to behave like an adolescent. In other words, there are conflicts:

"Je ne réalise pas l'unité structurale. La seule unité structurale que je me connais est l'unité du personnage social que je répresente, mais qui ne recouvre pas tout. Comment voulez-vous donc qu'il y ait une unité structurale chez l'enfant si elle n'existe pas chez l'adult?"

I would like, however, to approach the question of structural unity on the basis of clinical, developmental, and evolutionary speculation. Not that I could even begin to suggest methods of inquiry approaching the rigor demanded by Piaget, and exemplified in his synthesis of the experimental and the clinical. Most of us have our roots in one or the other, in the experimental or the clinical methods; that is, we know man either when he is well enough to lend parts of himself for study in suitable settings, or sick enough to fall apart into discernible fragments of behavior. The workers who turn to the first, the experimental method, are on the whole cautious in making any promises regarding their ability to reveal man's nature. But it is clear that their methodological modesty disguises the expectation that all their reliable data added together will eventually be equal to the total functioning of man—if, indeed, man could only be prevailed upon to realize that life would be much more manageable if he would consent to be the sum of his reliably investigated parts. I belong to another breed, the clinicians, who are modest and vain in different ways. Much less cautious, we speak with relative ease of the core of man's personality and of stages in its development. But then, our subjects want to become whole; and the clinician must have some theories and methods which offer the patient a whole world to be whole in. Mistaking our patients' gratitude for verification, we are sometimes sure that we could explain or even guide mankind if it would only consent to be our collective patient.

Piaget has been singularly successful in avoiding either of these illusions. The remark quoted was, of course, meant to pretend naïveté; and if I am not mistaken, he usually allows for such weakness in a discussion just before he turns politely but deftly on the clinicians present. At any rate, in his remark about his own behavior the terms "childlike" and "adolescent" should be in quotation marks. For Piaget would claim both too much and too little if he were to insist that what he refers to as a remnant of childishness is truly childlike, or his allegedly adolescent streak truly youthful. When "childlike," an adult may be surprisingly, or charmingly, or ridiculously childlike—for an adult; and when "adolescent," goodnaturedly or exuberantly or shockingly adolescent. But he is structurally an adult because his adulthood determines the nature and the use he makes of what is left of his earlier selves and what is presaged of his future ones, including his ability to remark on them in a sovereign and strategic manner.

Piaget's remark will serve, however, as an *illustration of a principle* which I wish to employ in charting the strengths of the ego at different stages of life—which are, of course, the structural basis of man's functional unity at such stages. I have used this principle of epigenesis in a number of other publications, in the form of a chart such as this:

Stage C	"childlike" adult	"adolescent" adult	adult adult
Stage B	"childlike" adolescent	adolescent adolescent	"adult" adolescent
Stage A	childlike child	"adolescent" child	"adult" child

Fig. 1

The child is childlike in Stage A, the adolescent adolescent in Stage B, and the adult adult in Stage C—in *this sequence*, for each stage represents a certain *period* during which (healthy) body and mind provide the *potentials* and the (true) community the corresponding *opportunities* for the accomplishment of such unity. Where processes of disease or disintegration upset this order, the childish or "childlike" adult would still be structurally different from a playing child; the precocious or "adult" adolescent different from an adult philosopher; and the unchildlike or "adolescent" child from an exuberant or brooding adolescent. However, we clinicians must admit that we understand crises typical for certain stages better than the stages themselves, and know the cubicles with the quotation marks better than those without. In psychoanalysis the stages of childhood were first identified with their typical inner crises, and their crises with the (mostly unconscious) instinctual wishes which gave them their urgency and provided their core-conflict. What man, at a given stage, had wanted unconsciously became that stage, and the sum of such stages, man; and even in Piaget's remark, reflecting somewhat of a caricature of clinical thinking, there is the suggestion that an adult who must admit that he harbors adolescent and infantile trends forfeits to that extent the claim of an adult structural unity.

It must be granted here that one is not an adult adult (nor was a childlike child, nor became an adolescent adolescent) without what Piaget calls conflict—a matter to which I would give a more normative and developmental status by calling it crisis. In fact, to each such unity corresponds a major crisis; and whenever, for whatever reason, a later crisis is severe, earlier crises are revived.

In presenting my schedule of emerging virtues, I have also implied, but not spelled out, the existence of developmental crises. I must briefly define this ancient little word. In clinical work (as in economics and politics) crisis has increasingly taken on half of its meaning, the catastrophic half, while in medicine a crisis once meant a turning point for better or for worse, a crucial period in which a decisive turn *one way or another* is unavoidable. Such crises occur in man's total development sometimes more noisily, as it were, when new instinctual needs meet abrupt prohibitions, sometimes more quietly when new capacities yearn to match new opportunities, and when new aspirations make it more obvious how limited one (as yet) is. We would have to talk of all these and more if we wanted to gain an impression of the difficult function—of functional unity. I have tried to take into account the double aspect of such crises by assigning double terms to the psychosocial stages which I have previously postulated.[10] Thus—to mention only three—infancy would culminate in a crisis in which basic trust must outweigh basic mistrust, adolescence in a crisis in which identity must prove stronger than role confusion, while in old age only integrity can balance despair. However, I will not deal in detail here with the psychosocial basis of those unifying strengths which I have called basic virtues.

It is not easy to admit, while speaking with some conviction of an evolving ground plan, that one does not yet know how to observe or to formulate its components. In this first attempt to name basic properties of the "strong" person (matters so far left to moralists and theologians), I have given these properties their everyday names: this is what they look like when observed in others; this is what they feel like when possessed; and this, above all, seems absent when "virtue goes out" of a person. Now, the negative of this kind of virtue cannot be vice; rather, it is a weakness, and its symptoms are disorder, dysfunction, disintegration, anomie. But "weakness" fails to convey the complexity of disturbance and to account for the particular rage which accumulates whenever man is hindered in the activation and perfection of the virtues outlined here. Only when active tension is restored, do things fall into place, strongly and simply. I, for one, remember with pleasure the

exclamation of a patient: "You sure know how to de-compli-
cate things!" Such flattery, however, is only as good as the
surprise behind it: one cannot pre-decomplicate things. In
this sense, the list of virtues only points to an order which, I
believe, will be found to be violated in every new form of
perplexing disorder and restored in its (always surprising)
resolution. To consider such order, then, is a matter of long
range study and contemplation: for the virtues seem to me to
point to principles of cohesion as well as to defects in the
"fiber" of generations and institutions.

To call hope in this context a vital virtue means only to
name that basic minimum without which the most highly valued and espoused hopes become irrelevant; it means to mark
the limits of the socio-genetic efficacy of all values. For values
which do not secure the re-emergence of the order of these
vital strengths (whatever their genetic disposition and their
individual nature) in each generation, are apt to lose—well,
their virtue.

In an epigenetic development of the kind here envisaged,
each item has its time of ascendance and crisis, yet each persists throughout life. Hope is the first and most basic and yet
it is also the most lasting; it is the most stable and yet acquires
new qualities, depending on the general stage reached. Thus,
in adulthood, hope may have become invested in a formulated
faith or endow an implicit one. Similarly, the rudiments of
will become part of an adult's determination, both in the sense
of his capacity to exert strong will over others and in his necessary self-control.

I would not be ready by any means to complete this list.
The point to be made is merely that what thus grows in steps
is part of an ensemble in which no part must have missed its
original crisis, its further metamorphoses, and its re-integra-
tion into each later stage. Thus, hope in infancy already has an
element of willfulness which, however, cannot be challenged
as yet in the way it must be when the crisis of will arrives in

the play age. That a baby already has some tiny developmental Anlage which will grow to become wisdom after a long life— that will be harder to defend against all but the most fanatic devotees of infancy. (On the other hand, Lao-tse, so I am told, does mean "old child . . .")

But it is true that the over-all stages of development in the human being cannot be grasped before what Piaget calls the "functional unity of the personality" is better understood. As human strengths, the virtues listed here are obviously super-ordinated to the psychosexual and psychosocial schedules, in the sense that they are an expression of their integration, even though the specific time within a stage, when such unity is reached, and the mechanisms by which it comes about are not yet known. What Freud calls oral libido obviously endows the experiences from which hope emerges. Both can only arise, and must arise, in infancy. On the other hand, oral libido would not find its place in the unity of the personality (and that means, as we have seen, in the unity of the generational process) without a strong and pervading hopefulness. This over-all state, however, depends on much more than a success-ful orality, even if there were such a thing as a successful libido on its own. It depends on the verifications, in social reality, of all the maturing part-functions of organism and mind. There is really no use, then, in asking what comes first: the ensemble arises with its parts and the parts with the en-semble; even though each part when first revealed by a new method may impress its finder as being the cause and the begin-ning of all other parts. Freud saw this when he called his in-stinct theory his "mythology." Myths do not lie, but they find new forms closer to observation.

WHATEVER IS BUILT into human development also has an evo-lutionary rationale. I have implied that I consider this to be true for the basic virtues. But the use of the word virtue in proximity to the term evolution immediately suggests one of the dreaded "naturalist fallacies." I use the word virtue in this context, however, not in order to read moral intentions into evolution, but in order to discern adaptive strengths which have emerged from it. Now it is obvious that man, who according to Waddington [11] "goes in for ethicizing," has built on the vital virtues moral and religious superstructures which impress us not only with their occasional capacity to lift man up but also to cause his frequent total downfall. For this very reason, however, we must recognize in human development that substructure and rockbottom of vital strengths which assure human adaptation from generation to generation. Geneticists hesitate to specify genetically transmitted "dispositions" by which man is born ready to negotiate with a social environment, not only for his full physiological stature and cognitive expanse, but also for a set of vital strengths which will make him the effective bearer of offspring, producer of tools, and carrier of tradition. Yet, Waddington recognizes not only that man "goes in for ethicizing," but that he is, by nature, an "authority acceptor." This, I think, will do as the minimum genetic acknowledgment necessary to assume inborn dispositions ensuring and negotiating sequences of generations living in organized societies. Within these processes, then, the vital virtues enumerated and tentatively named here are not lofty ideals (this they become, in fact, in their hour of relative weakness) but essential qualities arising from the convergence, in each life and in each generation, of unfolding capacities with existing institutions. If motherhood inspires hope, if ideological institutions provide grounds for fidelity, and if patterns of co-operation foster love, then each depends on the sequence of all, and all on some original total disposition emerging in that total cultural milieu, of which human motherhood is a part. The disposition, to be sure, is for Hope, not for a particular variety of prescribed hopes; it is for Fidelity and not for particular loyalties and devotions which, in fact, may sharply contrast with each other from ideology to ideology; it is for Love, and not for a particular cultural combination of love with sexual and social mores.

To complete my discourse in which the word evolutionary has appeared so regularly, I should admit that the thoughts which I am advancing here were partially provoked by a request from Sir Julian Huxley to contribute to a volume called, "The Humanist Frame." [12] For this he encouraged me to "write what you have long wanted to say," and what emerged is the scheme which I have presented here. To discuss further the dialectics of evolution and ego, I must reach back to the world-view, or better the world mood, which has emerged from both Darwin's and Freud's investigations, and which is to blame, I think, for our hesitation in studying human strength.

Darwinism and Freudian psychoanalysis have successively focused on what is popularly considered man's "lower nature": the descent and evolution of the genus man from a pre-human state of animality; the emergence of civilized man from degrees of savagery and barbarism; and the evolution of individual man from the stages of infantility. They have shown the relation of rational man's everyday irrationalities to insanity, and revealed political man's propensity for mob anarchy. Each of these insights at first met with derision and disbelief, but soon assumed the form of modern myths. Popular thought (and that includes specialists in non-biological fields) has generalized Darwin's theory as a "tooth-and-claw" struggle for survival, in which the crown of creation would go to what T. H. Huxley called the "gladiatorial" type of man. Similarly, popular thought (and that includes scientists not familiar with the advancements of psychoanalysis) has crudely over-simplified Freud's theory of inner conflict. It clings to the earliest formulation of this conflict and conceives of it as an inner tooth-and-claw struggle between ravenous instincts (the impersonal "Id") and cruel conscience (the moralistic "Super-Ego"). Thus the moral alternatives seemingly implicit in Darwin's and Freud's discoveries have been over-dramatized —as if mankind were taking revenge on these fearless men by forcing them into the role of tragic high priests in the cult of "facing man's lower nature," a nature which could now be faced with moralistic derision, or with an acceptance which soon excused everything. That double myth of an inner and outer struggle to the death has made it difficult for both biology and psychoanalysis to come to grips with the question of man's strength. Yet if man's future were dependent on his unbridled "instincts" or his overweening conscience alone, it could predictably end in species-wide suicide—in the name of the highest principles.

But the problem is not all one of popularization. The scientific (and ethical) necessity to view man's repudiated origins and his "lower nature" with an unflinching eye has led the scientific observer himself into an untenable dualism. G. G. Simpson, in the very conclusion of the book *Behavior and Evolution,* edited by him, makes reference to the essay on the evolution of human behavior by Roe and Freedman:

> With all this behind us, and with us, we are—who can doubt it? —sexual, aggressive, and acquisitive; in closing, my only regret is that Freedman and Roe intentionally omitted from this list the characteristic best exemplified in and by this book—exploratory curiosity.[13]

And indeed, the two authors of that essay, while lining up with admirable clarity all the data suggested by clinical observation, tend to attach to these data interpretations derived from psychiatric work, and describe man, as it were, with his "inside out," a nearly helpless victim of repression, conflict, and ambivalence. This endows the primates with an image of the infant reconstructed from clinical experience. Thus (as Simpson suggests), they seem to have forgotten themselves and excluded from evolution what they are doing when they write about evolution. Here, they have followed a tradition which characterizes psychoanalysis, as well. Freud's model of man consists primarily of the processes which he observed when, with such primeval courage, he looked into himself as he looked into his patients; but the model had no place for the judicious observer, the curious man. Science, morality, and himself Freud "took for granted."

Yet, both Darwin and Freud have given us the means to re-evaluate conscience itself, which was seen by Darwin as "by far the most important . . . of all the differences between man and the lower animals" yet solely devoted to "the welfare of the tribe—not that of the species, nor that of an individual member of the tribe." And it was Freud who revealed the instinctual crudeness and tribal cruelty in much of man's morality. History since Freud and Darwin has amply illustrated the limitations and dangers of a tribal conscience, especially when it is in the possession of modern technology.

Julian Huxley, at his best, summed the matter up at the end of his Romanes Lecture:

The peculiar difficulties which surround our individual moral adjustment are seen to be largely due to our evolutionary history. Like our prolonged helplessness in infancy, our tendency to hernia and sinusitis, our troubles in learning to walk upright, they are a consequence of our having developed from a simian ancestry. Once we realize that the primitive super-ego is merely a makeshift developmental mechanism, no more intended to be the permanent central support of our morality than is our embryonic motochord intended to be the permanent central support of our bodily frame, we shall not take its dictates so seriously (have they not often been interpreted as the authentic Voice of God?), and shall regard its supersession by some more rational and less cruel mechanism as the central ethical problem confronting every human individual.[14]

This passage expresses a view to which, in fact, psychoanalysis is dedicated both as a clinical technique and a system of thought. Every step in treatment and every act of clarification is directed toward the "supersession by some more rational and less cruel mechanism." This view is also well prepared for by an aspect of Freud's thought which has not provoked the imagination of other scientists as has his instinct theory: I refer to his ego-psychology.

Freud's concept of the ego is as old as psychoanalysis itself, and was, in fact, brought along from Freud's physiologic days. Freud first,[15] then Anna Freud,[16] and finally Heinz Hartmann [17] have worked consistently on the refinement of the concept. Yet, this "structural" part of Freud's work seems to have less appeal. Psychologists have continued to refer to the field of psychoanalysis as primarily concerned with the "affective," and biologists prefer to think of psychoanalysis as covering the sexual or, at best, the "emotional" only. It is obvious, I think, that the shock caused by Freud's earlier systemizations of the dichotomy of instinct and super-ego has been absorbed so slowly, and with so much emotional ambivalence, that Freud's later thoughts have simply not reached the attention of the majority of scientific workers. And even where the psychoanalytic concept of the ego has permeated, it has been immediately drawn into the imagery of man's "lower nature," and into the popular meaning of ego, namely, an inflated self. Thus a church-historian, in one of the best of our academic journals, could suggest that a psychoanalytic study of Luther's identity crisis was meant to show that Luther started the Reformation merely "for the satisfaction of his ego." To that extent has the popular "ego" as a designation of modern man's vain sense of a self-made Self (a precarious sense, subject to sudden deflation by the pricks of fate—and of gossip) penetrated the vocabulary even of the learned. But it happens to designate the opposite of the psychoanalytic meaning; therefore in all but the most specialized circles, it is still necessary to say what the ego is not.

The psychoanalytic meaning of ego designates it as an inner-psychic regulator which organizes experience and guards such organization *both* against the untimely impact of *drives* and the undue pressure of an overweening *conscience*. Actually, ego is an age-old term which in scholastics stood for the *unity* of body and soul, and in philosophy in general of the *permanency* of conscious experience. Psychoanalysis, of course, has not concerned itself with matters of soul and has assigned to consciousness a limited role in mental life by demonstrating that man's thoughts and acts are co-determined by unconscious motives which, upon analysis, prove him to be both worse and better than he thinks he is. But this also means that his motives as well as his feelings, thoughts and acts, often "hang together" much better than he could (or should) be conscious of. The ego in psychoanalysis, then, is analogous to what it was in philosophy in earlier usage: a selective, integrating, coherent and persistent agency central to personality formation. William James still used the term in this sense: in his letters, he speaks not only of "the ego's active tension," but also of the "enveloping ego to make continuous the times and spaces not necessarily coincident of the partial egos." [18] But then, his self-observation had brought him close to the study of impaired states in which the ego was first revealed in its weakness, and then recognized as a control regulator of remarkable endurance and power.

Psychoanalysis, then, while first concentrating on the vicissitudes of instinctual forces in man (as recognizable in clinical symptoms and universal symbolisms, in dreams and in myths, in the stages of ontogeny and the evolution of the species), never ceased its work in the second area of inquiry, namely, on that "coherent organization of mental processes" which, in this caldron of forces and drives, assures a measure of individuality, intelligence and integrity. Only the measure of the measure varied. The original awe of the inner conflicts which motivate man made his ego seem to be a pathetic compromiser between the Id, which had a monopoly on all instinctual fuel of man's "animal-nature" and the Super-Ego, which could claim the support of all-knowing priests, all-powerful parents, and all-embracing institutions. No wonder that, at the time, the ego seemed to Freud like a rider who is "obliged to guide (his horse) where it wants to go." Gradually, however, the study of the human ego, the guardian of individuality, revealed it to be the inner "organ" which makes it possible for man to bind together the two great evolutionary developments, his *inner life* and his *social planning*.

The ego was gradually seen to be an organ of active mastery, not only in defending the inviolacy of the person against excessive stimulation from within the organism or from the environment, but also in integrating the individual's adaptive powers with the expanding opportunities of the "expectable" environment. The ego thus is the guardian of *meaningful experience*, that is, of experience individual enough to guard the unity of the person; and it is adaptable enough to master a significant portion of reality with a sense, in this world of blind and unpredictable forces, of being in an *active state*. This means that a "strong ego" is the psychological precondition for that freedom which has alternately been specified as the effort through which the inevitable comes to pass—or the will to choose what is necessary.

But I must say in passing that over the years I have become less intolerant of the popular misunderstanding of the term "ego," for it covers, as folklore often does, a deeper truth. Up to a point, the ego can be understood as a guardian of man's individuality, that is, his indivisibility. But in the midst of other individualities, equally indivisible, the ego must guard and does guard certain prerogatives which man cannot afford to be without and which he therefore will maintain both with secret delusions (such as are revealed in his dreams and daydreams) and in those collective illusions which often guide his history. Some of these prerogatives are a sense of *wholeness*, a sense of *centrality* in time and space, and a sense of *freedom of choice*. Man cannot tolerate to have these questioned beyond a certain point, either as an individual among his fellow men, or as a member of a group among other groups. It is for this reason that in individual memories and in collective history man rearranges experience in order to restore himself as the cognitive center and the source of events. He has crowned all-powerful kings and created all-knowing gods, endowing them with all the ego-ism the individual cannot do without: a central position in violent events; a sense of having willed and created fate itself; a certainty of being eternal and immortal; a conviction of being able to know the secret of life; the ability of being totally aware of goings-on everywhere and of influencing whatever one wishes to change. To restore this necessity of ego-ism in his own little self, man has also found means (inspirational, artistic, toxic) to be "beside himself" in order to feel himself to be more than himself. With all due respect, I see the latest version of this inexorable inner need in those post-Darwinists who insist that man, now that he recognizes himself as a part of evolution, and may learn to steer some of it by dint of this recognition, becomes the crown and the goal of it instead of a creature who does well if he manages to restore or undo what he has upset and wrought in the tiny and dark corner that he, at best, can know. When faced with one of the customary apotheoses of man by an otherwise strict scientist, I am apt to remember the remark of a co-ed who expressed the depth of our darkness in the direct way reserved to women. Her escort had just mused aloud that life was a strange thing, indeed. There was a silence which he took for inspired consent. But she asked quietly: ". . . as compared with what?"

If the super-ego, then, has guarded man's morality but also has made him its slave, the ego, more adaptively, permits him a measure of human balance, yet not without dangerous illusions—dangerous, I should add, because of the destructive rage which accompanies their failure. In this sense, the basic virtues enumerated here have their illusory side which can develop into grand delusions of vain virtuousness, and lead to specific rages of disillusionment. Yet each is indispensable, and each is necessary for that ensemble which is man at his most balanced; while all in moments of humor and wisdom, in prayer, meditation, and self-analysis, can be charitably transcended.

But where, in animal nature, is the precursor of human ego? Man has always tended to project what he calls his own "animal nature"—that is, his id-superego split—on animals, comparing, for example, his ravenousness with the eating style of dogs, or his rage with that of provoked tigers. Whole "bestiaries" attribute to animals the lowest vices as well as the conflicts of man. A recent calendar relates a medieval view according to which a lion never overeats, adding, "and when he feels he might overeat, he puts his paw in his mouth to prevent himself." So here, too, man ascribes to the lion an inner life by which he becomes aware of an illicit wish and actively prevents himself from "giving in," even as our conscience struggles with our desires. On the other hand, our abysmal ambivalence leads us to see also our most exalted virtues in the image of animals: we are as courageous as lions, as meek as lambs, or we see in the quiet glance of a dark-eyed beauty the mysterious eyes of a doe. What we do not ascribe to animals, and are usually surprised to find in reports and in moving pictures made in their natural habitat, is a certain built-in balance, a restraint and discipline within their ecological niche of survival and activity. For an analogy to what we call ego, we may have to contemplate a certain chaste restraint and selective discipline in the life of even the "wildest" animals: a built-in regulator which prevents (or "inhibits") carnivorous excess, inappropriate sexuality, useless rage, and damaging panic, and which permits rest and play along with the readiness to attack when hungry or intruded upon. Similarly, different species of animals share environments with a minimum of mutual interference or distraction, each minding its own section of the environment unless, and until, vital interests prove to intersect. Thus, the state of the adapted animal is defined by what we might call *ecological integrity;* a combination of mutual regulation and reciprocal avoidance which safeguards adaptation within the characteristic environment and with other species sharing it. Man, who has evolved into a creature who is always in the process of readjusting to historical change in his man-made world, obviously over-reacts (in suffering, for example, from affect-incontinence as Konrad Lorenz has said): for him to live up, on his level, to the animal's adaptive integrity would call for a mutual regulation of inner motivation and technical-social invention which he seems to approach only during certain glorious but unpredictable periods. But whether for new glory or mere survival, he must now take his place more consciously in the succession of generations within his psychosocial universe.

We cannot overlook for a moment that so far in his history man has realized the blueprint of his potentialities only in fragments. There are many reasons for this. History records the triumphs of perfectibility attained in certain eras and areas, and presents us with examples of human perfectibility, transient and yet preserved in forms and words speaking to us with the utter presence which Rilke, in his *Duino Elegies,* ascribes to lovers: *"So weit sind's wir"*—"that much is truly ours." Thus we recognize the perfection of harmonious growth in the Greek realization of an excellent body and an excellent mind—a harmony counterpointed by the tragedies, and the death of Socrates. We recognize the perfection of charity in the words of Christ and of St. Francis, against the background of the last Passion. And we see the emergence of technological and organizational perfection in our time, reaching to the stars and preparing the stage for species-wide tragedy. But history has, on the whole and until recently, lacked both the method and the intent to demonstrate the dynamic relation between these triumphs and the inner distortions and social sacrifices imposed alike on elites and masses. With the possible advent of world democracy and with the necessity that every child born be a child chosen to be born and guaranteed by a world community an equal degree of opportunity, the function and the consciousness of history will change radically.

THE COGWHEELING STAGES of childhood and adulthood are, as we can see in conclusion, truly a system of *generation* and *regeneration*—for into this system flow, and from this system emerge, those social attitudes to which the institutions and traditions of society attempt to give unity and permanence.

This, then, is the most immediate connection between the *basic virtues* and the *essentials of an organized human community*: adults are organized (among other reasons) for the purpose of deriving from the collectivity and from its tradition a fund of reassurance and a set of methods which enable them to meet the needs of the next generation in relative independence of the vicissitudes of individual fate. Trustworthy motherliness, thus, needs a trustworthy "universe," and the religion of women can be observed to have a different quality from that of men. The womanly verification of faith lies less in a logic which permits action without guilt than in what the woman can do with faith itself, namely, give hope and establish trust in new humans.

Human strength, then, depends on a total process which regulates at the same time the *sequence of generations* and the *structure of society*. The ego is the regulator of this process in the individual.

To use, once more, hope as an example: the emergence of this vital quality can be seen as defined by three co-ordinates: the relation of the mother's motherhood to her own past childhood; the mother-child relation itself; and the relation of both to institutions providing faith in procreation. All three are set to augment hope: the mother's own past has left her with the wish and the necessity to pass on that hope which emanated from her mother(s) and from her culture. Her infant's hope, once awakened, maintained, and developed has the power to augment hope in all around him. At the same time, however, the adults entrusted with the maintenance of an infant's hope need some societal confirmation and restoration of hope, whether it is offered by religious ritual or inspired and informed advice, or both. Once given, this reassurance is reflected in the gradual transformation of the small individual's generalized hopefulness into a faith related to the predominant assumptions concerning the order of the universe. And as he grows up, he will not only become ready to transmit such faith (in the form of hope) to his progeny, but he will also contribute to the preservation or change of those institutions which preserve a tradition of faith.

What begins as hope in the individual infant is in its mature form faith, a sense of superior certainty not essentially dependent on evidence or reason, except where these forms of self-verification become part of a way of life binding technology, science, and new sources of identity into a coherent world-image. It is obvious that for the longest period of known history religion has monopolized the traditional formulation and the ritual restoration of faith. It has shrewdly played into man's most child-like needs, not only by offering eternal guarantees for an omniscient power's benevolence (if properly appeased) but also by magic words and significant gestures, soothing sounds and soporific smells—an infant's world. This has led to the interpretation that religion exploits, for the sake of its own political establishment, the most infantile strivings in man. This it undoubtedly does. Yet at the height of its historical function it has played another, corresponding role, namely that of giving concerted expression to adult man's need to provide the young and the weak with a world-image sustaining hope. Here it must not be forgotten that religious world-images have at least contained some recognition (and this is more than radical rationalism could claim until the advent of psychoanalysis) of the abysmal alienations—from the self and from others—which are the human lot. For along with a fund of hope, an inescapable alienation is also bequeathed to life by the first stage, namely, a sense of a threatening separation from the matrix, a possible loss of hope, and the uncertainty whether the "face darkly" will brighten again with recognition and charity.

Will, in turn, matures to be the ego's disposition over the strength of controlled drive. Such will-power, however, must join the will of others in such a way that drive remains powerful and resourceful in all, even as it is restrained by voluntary self-abnegation and ready obedience. The institution which gives "eternal" form to such judiciousness is the law. The judiciousness which governs the training of the small individual's willfulness in its infantile beginnings is thus carried on by the individual and, as a social demand, carried into institutions which guard the traditional and support a balance of leadership and followership, of privilege and obligation, of voluntary action and coercion. To its majesty organized man surrenders the disposition over the leftovers of willfulness in himself and in others, half hoping and half fearing that he himself may get away with small transgressions once in a while, even while watching his neighbors with coercive righteousness. The law's majesty, on the other hand, relies on interpretation, and ambiguous decision as well as ambivalent obedience remain its daily diminutions. Thus institutions, too, suffer from the past: from the phylogenetic past which, at a critical time, attempted to take an "eternal" principle out of the flux of time, and to transform it into a set of laws so formulated as to anticipate all future contingencies; and the ontogenetic past common to all citizens, namely, their "law training" in childhood and all its inconsistencies. Whether, as children, they learned to believe in justice because they had learned to admire judiciousness and to love righteousness, or to hate the willfulness of others, the law is now a requirement for ego-strength. Emotions as well as social logic will participate in the maintenance of a balance of privileges, obligations, and prohibitions.

The dependence of any institution on rejuvenation by the emotional investment of generations brings with it a persistent double danger. Even as the individual, in frantic search of his earliest hope-giving relationship, may end up lost in delusions and addictions, so are religions, when they lose their bonds with living ethics, apt to regress to the fostering of illusory and addictive promises or empty fantasy. And even as the individual, under the impact of his infantile training in domestic law and order, can become "compulsive," i.e., excessively controlled by and concerned with the mechanisms of inner control, so organized law can become machinery using the letter to subdue the spirit which was to be safeguarded. One can speak, then, of "sick" institutions, but only as long as one specifies the adaptive mechanisms which have bogged down in mere repetitiveness; and as long as one does not indulge in the assumption that psychiatric enlightenment as such will heal society.

It seems probable, then, that what we have called basic virtues emerging from the dealings of generations with each other have their counterparts in the spirit of those human institutions which attempt to formalize and to safeguard such dealings. Without seeking a simple correspondence within any one virtue and any institution, I would posit a mutual activation and replenishment between the virtues emerging in each individual life cycle and the strengths of human institutions. In whatever way we may learn to demonstrate this, virtue in the individual and the spirit of institutions have evolved together, are one and the same strength. From the stages and virtues such individual dispositions as faith, judiciousness, moral purpose, technical efficiency, ideological devotion, ethical responsibility and detached sagacity flow into the life of institutions. Without them, institutions wilt; but without the spirit of institutions pervading the patterns of care, love, instruction and training, no virtue could emerge from the sequence of generations. However there is no one-to-one connection between single virtues and single institutions, such as churches, law courts, or economic establishments.

A survey may suggest premature conclusions concerning a large area, details of which remain as yet inaccessible to more systematic approaches. But a "long view" may at least clarify where, in general, one is going. It seems beyond question to me that a theory which is "to glean from psychopathology contributions to normal psychology," must complement observations of childhood with a view of adulthood, supplement a theory of the libido with a conception of other sources of energy, and fortify a concept of the ego with insights into the nature of social institutions.

An attempt to construct a ground plan of human strength, however, could be accused of neglecting diversities, of contributing to the fetish of deadly norms, and thus to the undermining of the individual as a hero or a rebel, an ascetic or a mere person of singularity. Yet, the life processes will always lead to more diversity than we can comfortably manage with our insights, our cures and our aspirations. And so will man's reaction to the diversity of conditions. In the processes of socio-genetic change we can ascribe a long-range meaning to the idiosyncratic individualist and to the deviant as well as to the obedient conformist. True *adaptation*, in fact, is maintained with the help of loyal rebels who refuse to adjust to "conditions" and cultivate an indignation in the service of a *to-be-restored wholeness* without which psychosocial evolution and all of its institutions would be doomed. When Camus says that faith is sin, he says it in a form and in a context which forcefully suggests that he "cares" to relive and to restate faith beyond any compromise which, as a child, he was forced to accept.

Where do we stand?

In our time, for the first time, one human species can be

envisaged, with one common technology on one globe and some surrounding "outer space." The nature of history is about to change. It cannot continue to be the record of high accomplishments in dominant civilizations, and of their disappearance and replacement. Joint survival demands that man visualize new ethical alternatives fit for newly developing as well as over-developed systems and identities. A more universal standard of perfection will mediate more realistically between man's inner and outer worlds than did the compromises resulting from the reign of moral absolutes; it will acknowledge the responsibility of each individual for the potentialities of all generations and of all generations for each individual, and this in a more informed manner than has been possible in past systems of ethics.

As we have seen, the individual ego can be strong only through a mutual guarantee of strength given to and received by all whose life-cycles intertwine. Whatever chance man may have to transcend the limitations of his ego seems to depend on his prior ability, in his one and only life cycle, to be fully engaged in the sequence of generations. Thus, the study of those miracles of everyday life which we have attempted to describe as the emergence of basic virtues seems indispensable to an appraisal of the process man partakes in, of the stuff he must work with, and of the strength he can count on, as he attempts to give a more unified direction to his future course.

V

Psychological Reality
and Historical Actuality

Whenever the focus of insight shifts, traditional concepts demand pause and reconsideration. The following two lectures attempt to restate an old conceptual dilemma, such as is properly brought before an assembly of colleagues; they, therefore, assume an intimate or renewed acquaintance with certain of Freud's writings. These lectures are an expansion of an address delivered before the Sunday Plenary Session of the American Psychoanalytic Association, Midwinter Meetings, New York, 1961.

1. EGO AND ACTUALITY

AMONG THE STORIES of Freud's preanalytic years which assume a mythological quality in our training is the report of one of Charcot's evening receptions when the master, during a bit of shop talk about hysteria in women, "suddenly broke out with great animation: *'Mais, dans des cas pareils c'est toujours la chose génitale, toujours . . . toujours . . . toujours'* . . . I know that for a moment I was almost paralysed with amazement and said to myself: 'Well, but if he knows that, why does he never say so?' But the impression was soon forgotten; brain anatomy . . . absorbed all my interest." [1]

Since then psychoanalytic enlightenment has come full cycle and it is not sexuality that remains unmentioned at evening receptions. Heirs of radical innovation, however, carry a double burden: they must do together what the founder did in lonely years and also strive to keep ahead of the habituations which result from success. They may well, at intervals, ask themselves what they have come to know and what they on occasion say with "great animation," without pursuing it with the momentum of discovery.

One such item, I submit, is our knowledge of human strength. We have all heard psychoanalysts (including ourselves) in private conversations or in unguarded moments of clinical discussion, describe with wonder the evidence for some patient's regained health. Such evidence often seems hard to classify because it appears to have resulted from unexpected encounters "in the outside world" and from opportunities beyond our theoretical anticipations.

During a recent discussion in a small circle, Anna Freud made the observation that children who come to feel loved become more beautiful. Does libido, then, so the discussants wondered half-humorously, "jump" from one person to another? At any rate, our theory of inner psychic economy does not tell us what energy transforms the whole appearance of a person and heightens, as it were, his tonus of living. A similar dilemma was circumscribed by W. H. Auden in a book review [2] in which he pointed out how difficult it is for the psychoanalyst to conceptualize deeds in contrast to behavior, that is (to paraphrase him), to differentiate action which makes a memorable difference in the shared lives of many from such stereotyped private behavior as can be studied in clinical isolation. Is this an essential limitation of psychoanalysis? Can we conceptualize man only if he is fragmented in acute inner conflict, that is to say, retreating from or preparing for those moments when "his virtues . . . go forth of him?"

I frankly do not know whether I will confirm such limitations or point beyond them as I discuss, from a number of angles, my impression that our often half-hearted and ambiguous conceptualization of reality has resulted in a failure to account for important features of adaptive and productive action and their relation to the major phenomena of ego strength.

What do we mean when we speak of the recognition of and the adjustment to reality? Hartmann has formulated the reality principle as the "tendency to take into account in an adaptive way . . . whatever we consider the *real features* of an object or situation;"[3] and the psychoanalytic usage of the term reality was quite recently stated again by Loewald[4] as "the world of things *really existing in the outer world*." Freud's criteria of reality are (as Hartmann has not uncritically pointed out) "the criteria of science, or more correctly, those that find their clearest expression in science . . . which accepts as 'objective' what is *verifiable by certain methods*." The emphases are mine, but the statements clearly say that the psychoanalytic method by its very design attempts to further man's adjustment by helping him to perceive facts and motives "as they are," that is, as they appear to the rational eye. Yet, Hartmann has also clarified the limited applicability of such rationalism to human adaptation: "there is no simple correlation between the degree of objective insight and the degree of adaptiveness of the corresponding action."[5] And, indeed, radical rationalism could lead to a preoccupation so strenuous that it would expose man to the dilemma of that centipede which found itself completely immobilized because it had been asked to watch carefully which of its feet it was going to put forward next. If Hartmann's approach to these matters develops from the consideration of thought, attention, and judgment to that of action, he follows faithfully, although he expands it firmly, the course of psychoanalytic preoccupation with reality. But this thinking harbors such terms as "acting *in regard to* reality,"[6] "action *vis-a-vis* reality,"[7] and "acting *in the outer world*,"[8] (italics added). Maybe our habitual reference to man's environment as an "outer world" attests, more than any other single item, to the fact that the world of that intuitive and active participation which constitutes most of our waking life is still foreign territory to our theory. This term, more than any other, represents the Cartesian strait jacket we have imposed on our model of man, who in some of our writings seems to be most himself when reflecting horizontally

—like a supine baby or a reclining patient, or like Descartes himself, taking to his bed to cogitate on the extensive world.

I believe that we can undo this strait jacket only by separating from our concept of *reality* one of its more obscure implications, namely, *actuality*, the world verified in immediate immersion and interaction. The German word *Wirklichkeit*, often implied in Freud's use of the word *Realität*, does combine *Wirkung*, that is activity and efficacy, with reality. There is in fact, in Freud's papers on metapsychology a mysterious footnote promising a "later passage on the distinction between testing with regard to reality and testing *with regard to immediacy*" [9] (italics added). Freud's original term for what is translated as "immediacy" was *Actualitaet*. The editor of the *Standard Edition* adds that no reference to this seems to occur anywhere else; and that the footnote may be "one more reference to a missing paper."

I will not attempt to surmise what kind of differentiation Freud had in mind so long ago. I can only state the problem as I see it in our day. The term "actuality" will strike us with different connotations depending upon whether we are devotees of small or big dictionaries. The shorter the annotation, the more does "actual" mean the same as "real." "Actuality," thus, can be just another word for phenomenal reality, and yet its linguistic origin vouches for a reality due to a state of being actual, present, current, immediate. It is in the verbs "to activate" and "to actuate" that this meaning has most strongly survived, for what actuates "communicates motion," "inspires with active properties."

I intend here to make the most of this linguistic difference and claim that we must put into their proper relations—sometimes close to identical, sometimes directly antagonistic—that *phenomenal reality* which by psychoanalytic means is to be freed from distortions and delusions, and the meaning of reality as *actuality*—which is participation free (or to be freed) from defensive or offensive "acting out." *Reality*, then (to repeat this), is the world of phenomenal experience, perceived with a minimum of distortion and with a maximum of customary validation agreed upon in a given state of technology and culture; while *actuality* is the world of participation, shared with other participants with a minimum of defensive maneuvering and a maximum of mutual activation.

Mutual activation is the crux of the matter; for human ego strength, while employing all means of testing reality, depends from stage to stage upon a network of mutual influences within which the person actuates others even as he is actuated, and within which the person is "inspired with active properties," even as he so inspires others. This is *ego actuality;* largely preconscious and unconscious, it must be studied in the individual by psychoanalytic means. Yet actualities are shared, as are realities. Members of the same age group share analogous combinations of capacities and opportunities, and members of different age groups depend on each other for the mutual activation of their complementary ego strengths. Here, then, studies of "outer" conditions and of "inner" states meet in one focus. One can speak of actualities as co-determined by an individual's *stage of development*, by his *personal circumstances*, and by *historical and political processes*—and I will, in fact, speak of all of these.

The concept of activation is intimately related to one of the last dominant interests of the late David Rapaport, who left a paper in which he frees from the tangle of conflicting formulation the various meanings of the terms "activity" and "passivity," in order to formulate the ego's active and passive states. The ego's active state leads to integrated action while the ego's passive state is characterized by "helplessness in the face of drive demand" and by the "paralysis . . . of control." [10] I wonder whether it would not be better to leave the term passivity to other phenomena and to speak of the ego's *inactivation* rather than of its passivity as the state essential to all dangers to the ego. For passivity can be an active adaptation, while only inactivation results in paralysis. At any rate, it is the ego's very essence to maintain an active state not merely by way of making compromises with reality but by a selective involvement in actualities.

Here, it seems, an issue which first arose with the psycho-analysis of children awaits systematic clarification. I mean the assessment of variations of therapeutic technique not only from the point of view of the patient's "analyzability" but also from that of his adaptability, i.e., his chances of re-establishing active ego tension in his actuality. For it is clear that each stage of development has its own acuteness and immediacy, because a stage is a new configuration of past and future, a new combination of drive and defense, a new set of capacities fit for a new setting of tasks and opportunities, a new and wider radius of significant encounters. The truly recovering patient of any age must turn his powers of recognition toward fellows by whom he in turn will be recognized, and must direct his needs for activation toward those who in turn will be activated by him. As Shakespeare says (in *Troilus and Cressida*), man

> . . . feels not what he owns, but by reflection
> As when his virtues shining upon others
> Heat them, and they retort that heat again
>   to the first giver.

BUT BEFORE attempting to define *developmental actuality*, let me illustrate its clinical relevance by discussing a question which we have all asked ourselves at one time: what *was* it Dora wanted from Freud? [11]

When we use Freud's cases and dreams for the elucidation of what we are groping to say, it is for one very practical reason: all of us know the material by heart. Beyond this, we always find in Freud's writings parenthetical data worthy of the attention of generations to come. We must assume, of course, that Freud selected and disguised the clinical data he published, thus rendering reinterpretations hazardous. Yet, the repeated study of Freud's case reports strengthens the impression that we are dealing with creations of a high degree of psychological relevance and equivalence even in matters of peripheral concern to him. And Freud always made explicit where he stood and how far he had come. Thus, he concludes his report on the treatment of Dora with an admission as frank as it is rare in professional publications: "I do not know what kind of help she wanted from me."

Dora, you will remember, had returned to him a year after she had interrupted a treatment that had lasted only three months. She was twenty years old then and had come back "to finish her story and to ask for help once more." But what she told him then did not please Freud. She had in the interval confronted her family with certain shady events denied by all (I will come back to their nature), and she had forced them to admit their pretenses and their secrets. Freud considered this forced confrontation an act of revenge not compatible with the kind of insight which he had tried to convey to the patient. If she now knew that those events had caused her to fall ill, it was her responsibility to gain health, not revenge, from her insight. The interview convinced him that "she was not in earnest over her request" for more help, and he assured her that he was willing "to forgive her for having deprived [him] of the satisfaction of affording her a far more radical cure." Since Dora was intelligent, however, the judgment that she was "not in earnest" suggested insincerity on her part. And, indeed, Dr. Felix Deutsch who later—in her middle age and far from the scene of her first treatment—was consulted by Dora gives an unfavorable picture of her fully developed character—as unfavorable as any that may be seen in clinical annals.[12] What must interest us is that in Freud's original description of the girl, Dora appeared "in the first bloom of youth— a girl of intelligent and engaging looks." If "an alteration in her character" indeed became one of the permanent features of her illness, it seems possible that Dora may have been confirmed in such change by the discontinuance of her treatment.

The description of Freud's fragmentary work with Dora has become the classical analysis of the structure and the genesis of a hysteria. It is clear from his description that Freud's original way of working and reporting was determined by his first professional identity as a physiological investigator: his clinical method was conceived as an analogy to clean and exact laboratory work. It focused on the "intimate structure of a neurotic disorder"—a structure which was really a reconstruction of its origins and a search for the energies, the "quantities of excitation," which had been "transmuted" into symptoms, according to the dominant physicalistic configurations of his era. As to the unbearable excitations "transmuted" into Dora's symptoms, it will suffice to mention the two traumatic sexual approaches made to the girl by a Mr. K., a married man who kissed her once when she was fourteen under circumstances indicating that he had set the scene for a more thorough seduction; and who propositioned her quite unequivocally at an outing by an Alpine lake when she was sixteen. She had rebuked the man on both occasions, but her arousal and repugnance had been so violent that they led to hysterical symptoms which then were traced back by Freud to the sensations, affects, and ideas experienced in those events. This was his method; but how clinically alive and concrete is his question as to what more, or what else, Dora had a right to expect of him. He could not see, Freud relates, how it could have helped her if he "had acted a part . . . and shown a warm personal interest in her." He did perceive, then, an interpersonal distance in his method; but no patient's demands were to make him dissimulate his integrity as an investigator and his commitment to the truth: they were *his* criteria of the respect due to a patient.

If in the patient's inability to live up to his kind of truth

Freud primarily saw repressed instinctual strivings at work, he certainly also noted that Dora, too, was in search of some kind of truth. He registered the fact that the patient was "almost beside herself at the idea of its being supposed that she had merely fancied the conditions which had made her sick;" and that she kept "anxiously trying to make sure whether I was being quite straightforward with her." And, indeed, the girl had every reason to suspect the whole older generation of having conspired against her; had not her father asked Freud "to bring her to reason"? Freud was to make his daughter drop the subject of her attempted seduction by Mr. K. The father had good reason for this wish, for—and here we come to the suspicion of an erotic barter with which she subsequently confronted her family—Mr. K.'s wife was his own mistress, and he seemed willing to ignore Mr. K.'s advances to his daughter if he could remain unchallenged in his own affair.

Dora, no doubt, was in love with Mr. K. whom Freud found to be quite a presentable man. But I wonder how many of us can follow without protest today Freud's assertion that a healthy young girl would, under such circumstances, have considered Mr. K.'s advances "neither tactless nor offensive." The nature and severity of Dora's pathological reaction make her, of course, the classical hysteric of her day; but her motivation for falling ill, and her lack of motivation for getting well, today seem to call for developmental considerations which go beyond (although they include) the sexual conflicts then in the focus of Freud's studies.

As pointed out, Freud's report indicates that Dora was concerned not only with the recognition but also with the joint acknowledgment of the historical truth, while her doctor insisted on the psychic reality behind the historical truth: for, according to his view, only her own conflict between love and repugnance could explain the nature of her symptoms. At the same time she wanted her doctor to be "truthful" in the therapeutic relation, that is, to keep faith with her on her terms rather than on those of her father or seducer. That her doctor did keep faith with her in terms of his investigative ethos she probably appreciated up to a point; after all, she did come back. But why then surprise him with the fact that she had confronted her parents with the historical truth?

This insistence on action may impress some of us even today as "acting out." With Freud, we may predict that the patient would gain a permanent relief from her symptoms only by an ever better understanding of her own unconscious, an understanding which would eventually permit her to adjust to the "reality" both of the events and of her reaction to them, for neither could now be helped. And it is sometimes too easy to flee from psychic reality into historical proof of one's victimization. Strictly speaking, however, we could expect a full utilization of such insight only from a "mature ego," and Dora's neurosis was rooted in the developmental crisis of adolescence. The question arises whether today we would consider the patient's active emphasis on the historical truth a mere matter of resistance to the inner truth; or whether we would discern in it also an adaptive pattern specific for her stage of life, challenged by her special conditions, and therefore subject to consideration in her treatment. For we may suspect that at each stage of life, what appears to us as "acting out" may contain an adaptive if immature reaching out for the mutual verification by which the ego lives; and that, between adolescence and young adulthood, the pursuit of "the truth" may be of acute relevance to the ego's adaptive strength.

There are, of course, many ways in which a young person may express a sudden preoccupation with truth—at first perverse and obsessive, changeable and pretentious, and altogether defensive in Anna Freud's sense, but gradually taking hold of relevant issues and productive commitments. He may come to have a personal stake in the accuracy, veracity, and authenticity, in the fairness, genuineness, and reliability of persons, of methods, and of ideas. I have elsewhere postulated the quality of *fidelity* as the essence of all these preoccupations. As in adolescence, powerful new drives must find sanctioned expression or be kept in abeyance, and as wild regressive pulls must be resisted, it is a prime necessity for the ego that the capacity to pledge and receive fidelity emerge and mature during this period—even as societies, for the sake of their rejuvenation, must receive from their youth, by way of all manner of "confirmations," the pledge of particular fidelities in the form of ideological commitment.

Piaget and Inhelder,[13] who have studied the thought processes of adolescents by confronting them with certain experimental tasks, have recognized in adolescence the ripening of a mode of thinking both "hypothetical" and "deductive." That is: the adolescent, before beginning to manipulate the material at hand, as the pre-adolescent would do with little hesitation, waits and hypothesizes on the possible results, even as he lingers after the experiment and tries to fathom the truth behind the known results. This capacity forms, I think, a basis for the development, in later adolescence, of the *historical perspective*, which makes room not only for imaginative speculation about all that could have happened in the past, but also a deepening concern with the narrowing down of vast possibilities to a few alternatives, often resolved only by a "totalistic" search for single causes. Youth is, at the same time, preoccupied with the danger of hopeless determination, be it by irreversible childhood identifications, by ineradicable secret sins or socially "stacked" conditions, and with the question of freedom in many urgent forms. Where a sense of fatal predetermination prevails, the quest for its causes becomes an ideological one, defying a merely intellectual approach. Thus, what we would consider an interpretation to youth easily becomes a statement of doom. Patients such as Dora, therefore, may insist that the inner meaning of their sickness find recognition within an assessment of the historical truth, which separates that which has become irreversible from the freedom of opportunities yet undetermined.

The employment of the particular cognitive gains of any stage of life is thus not just a matter of exercising intelligence, for these gains are part of a new pattern of verification which pervades a person's whole being. We know in pathology that certain forms of psychopathic evasion and of truly psychotic denial must wait for the full establishment of historical perspective in adolescence. Only he who comprehends the nature of irreversible historical truth can attempt to circumvent or to withdraw from it.

If fidelity, then, is a central concern of youth, Dora's case appears to be a classic example of fatefully perverted fidelity. A glance back at her history will remind us that her family had exposed her to multiple sexual *infidelity* and *perfidy;* while those concerned—father and mother, Mr. K. and Mrs. K.— tried to compensate for it all by making Dora their *confidante,* each burdening her (not without her perverse provocation, to be sure) with truths and half-truths which were clearly unmanageable for an adolescent. It is interesting to note that the middle-aged Dora, according to Felix Deutsch's report, was still obsessed with infidelities—her father's, her husband's, and her son's; and she still turned everybody against everybody else. But lest it appear that I agree with those of Freud's social critics to whom Dora seemed only a case illustrating typical Viennese and bourgeois infidelity, I must add that other and equally malignant forms of fidelity-perversion can characterize late adolescent case histories in other societies and periods. The specific social and cultural conditions of her place and time, however, determined her milieu's confusing role demands. As a *woman,* Dora did not have a chance. A vital identity fragment in her young life was that of the *woman intellectual* which had been encouraged by her father's delight in her precocious intelligence, but discouraged by her brother's superior example as favored by the times. When Freud last saw her, she was absorbed in such evening education as was then accessible to a young woman of her class. The negative identity of the *déclassée* woman (so prominent in her era) she obviously tried to ward off with her sickness. Mr. K., at the lake, had tried to seduce her with the selfsame pleading, namely, that his wife left him unsatisfied, which had previously been successfully used with a domestic (who also had confided in Dora). She may well have sought in Mrs. K., whom Freud recognized primarily as an object of Dora's ambivalent homosexual love, that *mentor* who helps the young to overcome unusable identifications with the parent of the same sex: Dora read books with Mrs. K. and took care of her children. But, alas, there was no escape from her mother's all-pervasive "housewife's psychosis." I would, in fact, conclude that it was this identity fragment which Dora blended with her own *patient identity*. For we know today that if patienthood is permitted to become a young patient's most meaningful circumstance, his identity formation may seize on it as a central and lasting theme. And, indeed, Felix Deutsch reports that the middle-aged Dora, "chatting in a flirtatious manner . . . forgot about her sickness . . . displaying great pride in having been written up as a famous case." To be a famous, if uncured, patient had become for this woman one lasting positive identity element; in this she kept faith with Freud.

This brings us, finally, to the therapeutic relationship itself. At the time, Freud was becoming aware of the singular power of transference and he pursued this in his evidence. Today we would go beyond it. We know that this most elemental tie is always complemented by the patient's relation to the analyst as a "new person." This has been most forthrightly formulated by Loewald in a paper which anticipates much of my argument about the role of reality-testing within the actuality of the therapeutic relationship.[14] Young patients in particular appoint and invest the therapist with the role of mentor, although he may strenuously resist expressing clinically what he believes and stands for. His patient's demands do not obligate him, of course, to "play a part," as Freud so firmly refused to do. True mentorship, far from being a showy form of emotional sympathy, is always part of a discipline of outlook and method. No good therapist or teacher need protest "human" respect, personal friendship or parental love. But the psychotherapist must recognize what his role is in what we are here trying to circumscribe as the actuality of a young person.

We have used the question as to what Dora wanted from Freud to come closer to essential aspects of a young patient's actuality. To establish and share the historical truth may have been a need surpassing childish revenge; to call the older generation's infidelities by their name may have been a necessity before she might have been able to commit herself to her own kind of fidelity; to establish some of the co-ordinates of her own identity as a young woman of her class and time may have been a necessary prelude for the utilization of more insight into psychic reality; while the conviction of mutual trustworthiness may have been a condition for the toleration of the transference, whether she saw in her persistent doctor another seducer or another critical authority.

Beyond all this, however, we face here a problem of general therapeutic urgency. Some mixture of "*acting out*" and of *age-specific action* is to be expected of any patient of whatever age, and all patients reach a point in treatment when the recovering ego may need to test its untrained or long-inhibited wings of action. In the analysis of children, we honor this to some extent, but in some excessively prolonged treatments of patients of all ages, we sometimes miss that critical moment while remaining adamant in our pursuit of totally cleansing the patient of all "resistance to reality." Is it not possible that such habitual persistence obscures from us much of the ego's actuality, and this under the very conditions which would make observation possible on clinical homeground?

I HAVE SPOKEN earlier of fidelity and indicated that I consider it a pervading quality which matures during the stage of youth. On another occasion I have called this quality a basic virtue, and I would like to share with you briefly the kind of thinking which may motivate a psychoanalyst to use such a word.

"Virtue" has served different value systems for their various purposes. The Romans meant by it what made a man a man, and Christianity, what added spirit to men and soulfulness to women. It has lent itself to qualities of sternness and fortitude, of meekness, compassion, and self-denial. But it has always meant *pervading strength,* and *strength of efficacy*—not only shining, then, but "heating and retorting heat." I therefore put the word to our use to underscore the fact that only basic strength can guarantee potency to any value; that ego strength develops from an interplay of personal and social structure; and that it emerges, as do all human capacities, in stages of development—and, that is to say, stages of changing actualities.

Fidelity, therefore, cannot be integrated before the stage of youth, and this for all manner of maturational reasons (physiological, cognitive, psychosexual, and psychosocial) which I shall not repeat here. For the same reasons, however, it *must* mature in youth lest the individual ego suffer an unduly aggravated crisis or lasting damage. Such a virtue, then, is built into the schedule of individual development as well as into the basic structure of any social order, for they have evolved together. It may be brash to imply by the use of the very word virtue that a tendency toward *optimum mutual activation* exists in the ego and in society. But the concept of reality, or so it seems to me, already implies an optimum correspondence between mind and the structure of the environment. A patient, we say, is impaired in his testing of reality. But, we may now add, he is also inactivated in actuality; and we can help him grasp reality only to the extent to which we, within our chosen method, become actual to him. This, at any rate, I want to offer for our consideration.

I cannot discuss here my nominations for the corresponding criteria of ego vitality at other stages of the life cycle. To become plausible, each would have to be anchored in the psychosexual, psychosocial, and cognitive components of its stage of emergence and each given a specific place in the hierarchy of all the stages. But I assume that the anchorage of the first of these criteria, hope, in the experiences of the oral stage is clinically apparent, and that the role of a lack or loss of hope in all the disturbances related to that stage is familiar to us. In passing, however, I would like to raise a question which is fundamental to the assumption of the stage by stage development of man's central strength. If the newborn infant brings with him to this life the pervasive quality that insures what is waiting for him (and relying *on* him) in the needs and drives of individual women, in the tradition of generations of mothers, and in universal institutions of motherhood, does it really make sense to speak of an infant's rudimentary ego as being "weak" and to liken it to what is weak in an isolated adult's neurotic dependence? Why burden infancy with the prototype of a weak ego and adulthood with the utopia of a strong one? It is here that our traditional concept of reality fails to account for the fundamental fact that the infant, while not yet able to grasp and to test what we call our reality, is competent in his actuality. True, all beginnings are characterized by vulnerability, but as long as vulnerability is accompanied by an active adaptation to protective conditions, it is not a state of weakness. Actuality at all stages rests on the complement of inner and outer structure. Ego strength at any level is relative to a number of necessities: previous stages must not have left a paralyzing deficit; the stage itself must unfold under conditions favorable to its potentials; and maturing capacities must evoke co-operative responses in the *Umwelt* backed up by conditions necessary for joint survival. This, then, is *developmental actuality*. It depends at every stage on active, selective principles being in charge, and enabled to be in charge by an *Umwelt* which grants each stage the conditions it needs.

I cannot conclude these developmental remarks without expressing the belief that considerations of this kind will clarify what clinical and genetic observation can contribute to a future ethics—ethics not based on the moral injunction of avoiding affront to the ideal but on the ethical capacity to provide strength in the actual.

I WILL NOW TURN from one of our classical approaches, the case history, to another, the study of dreams, and will try to indicate how what I have said may help clarify (and thus be clarified by) our nightly return to past actualities. This will offer an opportunity to submit some of the assumptions concerning the various schedules of human development to our traditional testing ground, the interpretation of dreams. I will choose as the initial material some of Freud's dreams as presented and analyzed in the *The Interpretation of Dreams*; and I begin with the confession that it is easier for me to recognize the criteria of the life stages in some of Freud's dreams than in those of my patients or my students. Why should this be so?

Every trained psychoanalyst has studied Freud's dreams during the formative years of his training and has usually, more or less consciously, seen in them something more than, or different from, what his instructors saw. Often, what he saw contained a theoretical change he was to formulate much later, for Freud's dream productions are suggestive far beyond the points Freud himself made explicit in first reporting them. For the same reason, one sometimes thinks that one has learned from Freud what he has not really made explicit—while also, of course, continually rediscovering points mentioned by Freud only in passing. Beyond this, Freud's dreams suggest themselves for further analysis for the same reason for which he chose to publish them. He spurned the use of his patient's dreams because he considered them—or thought his readers surely would consider them—too abnormal for the illumination of what is most basic to dreaming, that most fanciful and yet most normal production of the human mind.

There are a number of other advantages in the use of Freud's dream-reports which would be hard to match in any other body of dreams: they are offered as a series, dreamed during one period of a life now known in much more detail than is usual in biography. Even their purpose, namely, to serve analysis, is acknowledged. At any rate, no one of us would undertake to present his own dream life to his colleagues as illustrations of normality.

I will claim that among the "latent" trends in Freud's data are matters pertaining to the stages of life which begin to reveal their outlines to us today. Since much of this is to be found in the manifest dream, or rather, in a continuum reaching from the formal surface to the unconscious content, it will not be necessary for me to indulge in the sport of newly interpreting what might be presumed to have been unconscious to Freud himself. Quite on the contrary, my evidence rests rather on the fact that Freud, while focusing on matters of his concern, and admittedly leaving out much that he considered irrelevant enough to be kept from the gossipy public, yet sketched into the general outline of his material what is relevant for our contemporary trend of investigation. For our purposes, however, it will be necessary to re-translate strategic passages.

Our first example is the first part of Freud's dream of The Three Fates (*Parzentraum*).[15] This dream occurred after a day of traveling and after an evening when Freud had to "seek his bed" (*das Bett aufgesucht*) without an evening meal —tired and hungry. We will review this dream, then, and ask this question: if in the analysis of a dream we come to the conclusion that it reaches back into problems of the *oral stage*, do we find evidence for the assumption that the dream, besides references to *food*, to *mouth* and *skin*, and to modes of *incorporation*, also concerns itself with the psychosocial problem of *basic trust*, with the first vital virtue of *hope*, and with the *cosmic order?*

Here is Freud's dream:

I went into a kitchen in search of (*um mir geben zu lassen*) some pudding. Three women were standing in it, one of them was the *hostess* (*Wirtin*) of the inn and was twisting (*drehen*) something about in her hand, as though she was making *Knodel* (dumplings). She answered that I must wait till she was ready. [These were not definite spoken words.] I felt impatient and went off with a sense of injury (*beleidigt*—insulted).

This, then, is the first part of the dream which will serve as our main illustration, the second part being less clear both in its manifest form and in the extent of Freud's associations. That a hungry sleeper dreams of a kitchen marks the dream as a manifestly "oral" one, although we must remind ourselves that an orality aroused by actual and acute alimentary frustration is different from the orality of a pathologically regressed dreamer to whom all frustrations of the day turn into insults on the oral level. But the fact is that here a personality not more regressed than that of any dreamer has faced an acute oral problem just before going to sleep, and is apt, therefore, to meet this problem in his dream with the resources of a well functioning ego. This permits us to ask whether in the total context of the dream report—i.e., the dream itself and the dreamer's "associated" afterthoughts—our criteria for the first stages of all the developmental schedules are discernible. In its manifest form the dream suggests much of the imagery and the peculiar tension of an *oral crisis:* the locality is that part of a house in which food is prepared; the mode of approach is demanding receptivity—for contrary to the translation, which pictures the dreamer as being "in search of food," the German original says that he goes there in order to let somebody give him food ("*um mir geben zu lassen*"); the dream population consists of women exclusively, and one of them is the *Wirtin*—a designation which every connoisseur of German song will recognize as the prototype of the food-and-drink-dispensing, all-maternal and yet on occasion romantic woman, who invites the lonely wanderer to her table, at least.

This hostess is twisting something about in her hands as though she were making dumplings and, as the dream said, she answers that the dreamer must wait until she is ready. Here, of course, we have the all important *delay* which must be faced in the oral stage and which exposes the child to tests of faith as to whether it can trust or learn to trust that the "hostess" will finally come and bring him his food on time, or whether she will leave him to the gnawing pain of his empty stomach. And, indeed, in a manner obviously childish, the dreamer feels impatient and goes off with a sense of injury, that is, with that pessimistic *sulkiness* which can be characteristic of a certain oral type in broad daylight.

Before reviewing Freud's associations, we may, in a didactic manner, list the inventory of our expectations concerning the not directly oral imagery and the psychosocial attitudes characterizing the stage of life to which orality properly belongs. The *bipolar relationship* to the mother we have already recognized: she, at that stage, is all of the comprehensible world, and therefore becomes, and in many ways remains, the model for the powers which, because they can give, can also withhold everything.

The *psychosocial crisis* of infancy decides the degree of dominance of a *sense of trust* in spite of all the mishaps, delays, and sudden estrangements which give the infant reason to mistrust the maternal persons. It is clear enough that the dreamer prefers deliberate *mistrust* to unsure trust. He refuses to wait and leaves the scene—to turn elsewhere and, in fact, to men, as will be seen in the dream's second part. We cannot say that he abandons *hope*, which we have designated as the *vital virtue* to develop in the oral state, for he obviously directs his hopefulness elsewhere and away from the sources of edible nutriment.

To complete the inventory of orality, we must also consider its *psychopathology*, that is, the symptomatology in neurosis, psychosis, and character malformation which indicates a malignant failure of the oral stage. Here we think of *delusion*, which turns to a fictitious reality; of *addiction* which seeks supplies of intense but shortlived hope in toxic substances; and of paralyzing *depression*, in which hope is abandoned altogether. And indeed, all of these we find in Freud's associations.

Freud's first association takes him back to the first novel which he read at the age of 13—the age (we note in passing) at which the young Jew is received into the religious community of men through the ritual of the Jewish confirmation. The hero of that novel, the dreamer reports, went mad and kept calling out the names of the three women who had brought both the greatest happiness and the deepest sorrow (*Unheil*) into his life—a *delusional psychosis*, then, the malignant expression of hopelessness. The fact that there were three women in the novel reminds the dreamer, in turn, of the three Fates, who "spin the destiny of man." It becomes quite clear to him then that one of the three women, namely, the inn hostess in the dream, "was" his mother. Love and hunger, he reflects, meet at a woman's breast; thus preparing (we add) the great alternative of basic psychosocial attitudes, trust and mistrust, which the maternal environment must balance in favor of trust and thus of lifelong *hope* in a benevolent fate.

The dreamer's second association also goes back to infancy when fate can cheat you before you know it. He remembers the remark of a man, who on seeing the good-looking woman introduced to him as his erstwhile wet-nurse, regrets the fact that he did not make better use of his opportunities.

Finally, the third association goes back to a childhood memory which the dreamer now recognizes as most decisive for the dream. He reports that at the age of six (the age of going to school) his mother tried to convince him of the biblical claim that we are all made of earth and all must return to earth by rubbing the palms of her hands together (like the hostess in the dream) and showing the child "the blackish scales of epidermis" as a proof of her own composition of an earthy substance. Here it is important to see that the very *origin of man*, and, in fact, the origin of living matter is at stake, and that the mother, the source of life-giving food and of hope-giving love, herself demonstrates the fact that her very body is created of dead matter, of earth and of dirt. And, indeed, the dreamer associates to this what he believes to be the saying "you owe *nature* a death," whereas Shakespeare really says, "Thou owest God a death." The associating dreamer thus puts nature, that is, a maternal figure, in the place of God, implying that a pact with maternal women is a pact—with death.

IN THE SECOND PART of the dream one lone man appears, and no women. After some altercations, a stranger and the dreamer become "quite friendly with each other"—which "ends the dream." Taking all of Freud's hints together, the second part of the dream suggests to me an investiture theme. At any rate, the manifest content and the associations suggest that its meaning is just this: that the dreamer turns from the women who have disappointed him to a man with whom he becomes friendly. The associations, as we will see, picture father figures who gave young Freud more substantial hope primarily by taking the intelligent boy into their community of learning. Note that the associations already mentioned recall the age of thirteen, that is, the age of confirmation, and the age of six, the school age—and remember that the teachers of European boys then were all men. If the first part of this dream, evoked by hunger, goes back to the actuality of the first stage of life, the second part leads (as I think all successful dreams do) forward again; for it obviously promises to the sulky dreamer autonomy from women and participation in the world of intellectual skills. However, I will restrict myself in the following to those of the dreamer's associations which amplify the original, the oral, themes.

A number of men come to the dreamer's mind, and all of them have names reminiscent of food. One such name is Knoedel, which means dumpling; another, Fleischl, which means flesh. From here associations bring the dreamer to his own name, which, so he complains without specification, has given people the opportunity for more or less witty remarks. To one conversant with German, the most obvious kind of low wit which could misuse Freud's name would be a reference to *Freudenhaus* and *Freudenmaedchen* ("house of joy" and "girl of joy"), which mean whorehouse and whore: a reflection, then, on women of his name. And, indeed, he recalls a witticism which was perpetrated on Goethe by his friend Herder, who in a poem asked him whether his name reflected a descent from Gods, from the Goths, or *"vom Kote"* which means earth, mud, or even feces. All of this, obviously, is equivalent to a dream oath: if your own mother is made of earth or dirt, or worse, and if your own name is like a curse, you cannot trust mother, origin, or fate: you must create your own greatness. And, indeed, all the dreamer's associations concerning men converge on the great Vienna Institute of Physiology in which, so the dreamer says, he spent the happiest hours of his student days—a happiness characterized, as he now associates, by the spirit of Goethe's poem:

> *Und wird Dich an der Weisheit Bruesten*
> *Mit jedem Tage mehr geluesten—*

which asserts that the "breasts of Wisdom" promise an eternal pleasure ever renewed and ever increasing, for the thirst after knowledge is not only sublimated desire, it is also related to the actuality of the predictable world, and thus gives man the autonomous power to change that world. Here, then, we have the sublimation of all that oral desire which in the dream appears with such immediate needfulness, and its displacement and application to the Alma Mater, the Mother of Wisdom who gives you more than perishable gifts, and provides you with the means to make something of yourself, to *change your fate.*

But here, too, the dreamer's associations warn of incautious intake and, in fact, *addiction*. As so often in Freud's dreams, he remembers cocaine, which he once helped introduce into local anesthesia, before its addictive qualities were known. But one thing was known: cocaine "takes *hunger* away." It is, of course, the very function of the basic mistrust, which orality also bestows on every healthy human, to prevent the all too trustful incorporation of bad substances. But the danger of *too* much mistrust is the inhibition of the wish to take. Thus, the dreamer feels that the dream warns him never to neglect an opportunity, but always to take what one can even if it involves doing a small wrong. The second part of the dream, then, emphasizes the turn from dependence to self-help, from women to men, from perishable to eternal substances, and ends with a friendly affiliation with a man with a pointed beard—a paternal teacher figure.

In summary, a hungry sleeper—and we should add, one who loves good food—abandons himself to the frustrations of the earliest stage of life when hunger was first experienced, and to the anger over unreliable women and whatever is too perishable, too mortal, and too dangerous to be relied upon. It should be pointed out again that this is not an "oral" dream in a regressed dependent, hopeless, or foolishly hopeful sense. It successfully graduates from orality to turn resolutely away from the mother and to transfer all trust to more autonomous situations. The dreamer's ego, consequently, appears in no way "regressed"—a term often thoughtlessly used when speaking of a dream's return to infantile wishes and frustrations. Rather, the dreamer returns to his earliest dealings with (and subsequent reiterations of) one of life's major themes, and he thinks himself forward again, through a number of stages, convincing himself that each mournful loss and each frightening graduation brings with it an increased autonomy and an enhanced ability to find in adult actuality the resources of competence and tradition.

Thus, the dream of The Three Fates illustrates the way in which the dream life reaches down from the actuality of the day to the earliest stages of life when disappointments and unfulfilled promises were experienced which have remained forever ready to be reactualized; and the way in which the dream retraces its steps "back up" to the dreamer's actuality.

2. INFANTILE AND HISTORICAL ACTUALITY

I WILL NOW COMPARE the infantile actualities rearoused in the dream of The Three Fates with those apparent in the dream of Count Thun—and then proceed to a review of the dreamer's adult actuality. But at this point it may be well to chart (if all too systematically) what we have found in the "oral" dream of The Three Fates and what we may expect to find in dreams leading back to other stages of infantile development (see Figure 2 on page 186).

Freud's dream following his encounter with the Austro-Hungarian prime minister Count Thun [16] offers a rare and yet representative example not only of the reactivation of an infantile stage but also of the interplay of infantile and political themes in adult dream life.

The acute stimulus for the dream of Count Thun is a clearly circumstantial and a clearly *anal-urethral dilemma*. Freud was asleep in a railroad compartment which lacked a lavatory; his dream was in response to a urinary need which eventually awakened him. Freud must admit, however, that he "usually is not awakened by physical needs" and that his needfulness as well as his dream belong in a special context for which he offers an extensive preamble. The circumstances prove to be especially apt to demonstrate the increasingly vulnerable state of the ego as the day necessarily brings evidences of its limitations and as both body and mind need restful conditions for their work of recovery. The evening before, Freud, accord-

Psychosexual Stage	Organ Mode	Psychosocial Stage	Rudiment of Ego-Strength	Related Psychopathological Mechanisms	Related Elements of Social Order
Oral-sensory-cutaneous	Incorporative	Basic Trust vs. Mistrust	Hope	Psychotic Addictive	Cosmic Order
Muscular-anal-urethral	Retentive-eliminative	Autonomy vs. Shame and Doubt	Will	Compulsive Impulsive	Law and Order
Phallic-locomotor	Intrusive	Initiative vs. Guilt	Purpose	Inhibitive Hysterical Phobic	Ideal Prototype

Fig. 2

ing to the English version, "had arrived" on the platform of the station while an earlier train was still standing there. The German original (*gehe aber schon*) indicates that Freud had gone to the platform early—in fact, before he was permitted to by regulations—in order not to miss his train, possibly under the influence of the "railroad phobia" which was one of his outstanding neuroticisms. However, he was going on his summer vacation and felt exuberant over the expected freedom from daily routine.

As he waited for his train, Freud saw Count Thun arrive at the station and observed how, in a high-handed manner, the prime minister waved the ticket inspector at the gate aside and "walked straight through the entrance." Count Thun was, according to a footnote, "an upholder of Bohemian self-government as against German nationalists," and strange as it now seems, Freud in his student days had been somewhat of a German nationalist within the Austro-Hungarian Empire.

After the prime minister's train left the station, Freud admits he ought "by rights" to have left the platform and returned to the waiting room. With "some trouble," however, he "arranged" permission to stay on the platform. The motivation for this insistence on special privilege may, again, have been his "railroad phobia," possibly compensated for by the very mood of willfulness which he then describes.

Having claimed unequal rights for himself, Freud was then on the lookout for anybody who might exercise some sort of "pull," humming in the meantime a tune from *Figaro* which expresses defiance of a count (*"Will der Herr Graf . . ."*). Already in a combative mood when he arrived at the station, he indulged in all kinds of insolent daydreams, not failing to remember Count Thun's popular nickname, Count Nichtstun (Count Do-Nothing), as well as the fact that the Count, who behaved so autonomously, was *not* going on vacation, but was only heeding the call of his vacationing emperor.

Freud finally secured a first-class compartment for himself

but, alas, one with no available lavatory. Complaint was of no avail; and Freud's only come-back was the suggestion, made to the platform master, that the Imperial Railroads might at least have holes sawed in the floor of such compartments.

How much the circumstantial restriction on his free will in the matter of using or not using a toilet riled the traveler can be seen from the fact that Freud confesses to an habitual depth of sleep very rarely disturbed by physical needs; while that night he woke up (out of the dream to be reported) at a quarter to three in the morning with a pressing need to urinate. In other words, in the rebellious mood in which he had commenced the trip, the railroad's injustice in providing unequal opportunities for physical relief became a personal injury calling up significant memories.

The preamble to the Count Thun dream, then, is an admirable model for the description of a dreamer's total situation. Instead of dwelling on its particular Victorian and Austrian elements, we would do well to observe how in a few masterful strokes this preamble introduces the historical conditions, the social status, the professional circumstances, the dominant mood, and the threatening physical need which altogether are to determine the dream to be dreamed or to be analyzed. At the same time, we note that all these different sections of life already have a common denominator in the actuality of the second psychosexual stage, namely, the anal-urethral one. To be sure, the dreamer's initial mood and condition is one of unrestricted male autonomy and initiative, made relative only by the awareness of the superior privilege with which the Count forced his way through the station entrance, as though the Imperial Railroads belonged to him. The comparison of his own freedoms with those of the prime minister begins that series of painful thoughts (we do not know what may have introduced the trend earlier that day) which are apt to wound a man's self-esteem and show up his overweening ego's vulnerabilities.

The dream itself is a long and a complicated one. The first

part of the dream attempts to maintain the impudent mood of the evening: the dreamer finds himself in a meeting of students such as he had attended in the days of fervent ideological interest in German nationalism. Anywhere in Europe, a meeting of students is a meeting of potential rebels and rabble rousers, and in the multi-national Austro-Hungarian Empire students were in the forefront of a number of *separatist* and *autonomist* movements. And, indeed, in the dream itself, another Count appears, also one who had favored some degree of autonomy for some part of the empire. Challenged to say something about the Germans, he contemptuously refers to their favorite flower, (which the dreamer thinks is called *pissenlit* in French), whereupon the dreamer "fires up," surprising himself with his anger. In the German original, "I fire up" is *"ich fahre auf,"* and can also mean a kind of violent startle such as may awaken a sleeping person. But the dream merely changes its locale, as it will proceed to do several times.

The dream has several distinct parts which are clearly differentiated from one another. I will use this opportunity, however, to demonstrate the way in which the method of mode-analysis shows the linking of the various dream parts by the *eliminative mode*. In doing so, I am not overlooking the fact that the dream also has dominant phallic and intrusive elements. For the dream only gradually declines from a general mood of phallic-exhibitionistic impudence, locomotor abandon, and uninhibited initiative, that is, from a "megalomanic" sense of being in control to the acknowledgment of a state of being controlled and a resulting sense of shame and anger. The dreamer's ego eventually regains its active state, but not without energetic attempts, in each part of the dream, to control the controlling forces which are, alternately, the eliminative urge and restrictive persons. Each part of the dream ends with the arousal of an affect or, at any rate, an increased self-awareness, which probably suggests that the dreamer was close to awakening. That the first such arousal should follow the suggestion of *"pissenlit"* makes sense in view of the dreamer's pressing circumstances. True, the need to urinate may itself have been perversely aroused by the circumstances. But here as in the succeeding parts of the dream, the dream fulfills its function of guarding sleep by shifting its locale, almost as if making a new effort. But each time, the "pressing need" makes itself felt again and is translated into spatial images and social situations which are to assure the dreamer that he is as yet master of his sphincters and is escaping the supervision of authorities. To understand this, however, one must accept the dream's tendency to play with spatial modalities, and to project inner bodily needs on the visualized surroundings. We have learned to observe this in the play of children and I will, therefore, point out the ingenious way in which Freud's dream manages this feat, although I am aware of the fact that this technical game will seem somewhat farfetched to all but those who have concentrated their attention on the interpretation of play and dream. To put it briefly: the eliminative mode of the urethral zone and the necessity of finding refuge in a locality of relief ("locus") are here expressed in a *need to pass through some exit* and *the need to reach some end station*. The delaying or forbidding authority, however, is represented—according to the social experience of the European middle-class child—by hired individuals.

In the second part of the dream, then, the dreamer is possessed by the "need to pass" through disputed rooms and "escape" through the exit of a building. I must point out, however, that the English translation does not facilitate the understanding of this eliminative complex. Dream documents (as historical ones) must always be re-examined for meanings lost in translations of different theoretical orientation. In this second part of the dream the locality is the Aula, the auditorium of the university; the doors are said to be "cordoned off." In the original German the word is "*besetzt*" (literally "sat upon") —a word well known indeed to all German-speaking children, for it adorns the doors of public toilets when they are "*oc-*

cupied," and thus, has signified to many a child under acute bowel pressure that he had to wait his turn. This allusion helps to mark the necessity to "escape" as well as the "need to pass" as related to an eliminative need. The "need to pass" in addition, is disputed by a housekeeper who offers to accompany the dreamer with a lamp, again suggesting a *Kinderfrau* or the European *Abortfrau,* the keeper of the keys in public toilets. The dreamer is proud of the cunning by which he passed by the person who was thus blocking his way, and turned a situation threatening to control his "exit" into one in which *he controls the control,* and thus gains autonomy and freedom of movement. This sense of cunning (as pointed out, an increased self-awareness comparable to the startle in the first part of the dream) possibly accompanied a tendency to give in to the physical "need to pass." Here the dream scene shifts again.

The "need to pass" is now transferred to a locality of different structure and yet of corresponding configuration. The dreamer feels even in his dream that the need to "escape out of town" only replaces the previous one of "getting out of a house." The corridors are replaced by railway lines, and the delaying personage by a cab driver (a *"Fiaker,"* to Viennese). The dreamer asks him half haughtily, half pleadingly to drive him to a certain *"Endstation."* But, alas, all the stations are again "cordoned off," that is, *"occupied."* So the dreamer becomes reflective again: he "decides" to try elsewhere.

In the fourth part, the dreamer finds himself in a setting more similar to the one in which he actually is, namely, a suburban train compartment; and, it seems, an affect more appropriate to his actual condition is now aroused, namely, embarrassment. There is something sticking in his buttonhole that exposes him to ridicule, or at any rate, public attention. Obviously, the impudent, active, and cunning tenor of the dream, and with it, the dreaming itself is in trouble. The dreamer now becomes conscious not only of his own reflection, but also of being observed, and the dream must shift again.

I have paraphrased the first four sections of the dream for the sake of an exercise which may have been somewhat too strenuous all around. I will now quote the last part of the dream, the grand and desperate finale, in which the dreamer tries to project the urethral body zone, his pressing eliminative need and the shame adhering to his ridiculous position onto the great figures of his lifespace: his father and—by association—emperor and God.

Once more I was in front of the station, but this time in the company of an elderly gentleman. I thought of a plan [*erfinde*] for remaining unrecognized; and then saw that this plan had already been put into effect. It was as though thinking and experiencing were one and the same thing. He appeared [*stellte sich*] to be blind, at all events, with one eye, and I handed him [*halte ihm vor*] a male glass urinal (which we had to buy or had bought in town). So I was a sick-nurse and had to give him the urinal because he was blind. If the ticket-collector were to see us like that, he would be certain to let us get away without noticing us [*als unauffaellig*]. Here the man's attitude [*Stellung*] and his micturating penis appeared in plastic form. (This was the point at which I awoke, feeling a need to micturate.)

The dreamer, we see, now finds himself back in front of the station, but this time in the company of an elderly gentleman. He now invents (for the German says "*erfindet*") a plan for remaining unrecognized, and, in fact, to become inconspicuous (for the German says "*unauffällig*"). At this point it is "as though thinking and experiencing were one and the same thing," his cunning now having reached the height of full coincidence of wish and actuality. The English translation, "I handed him a male glass urinal," however, disguises a most significant double meaning. The German, "*Ich halte ihm vor*," can mean "I hold something in front of him" or "I reproach him for something," as can the analogous phrase in English: "I hold something against him." This is not a negligible double meaning, for Freud tells the whole dream in order to demonstrate the importance of a childhood event when he had been reproached by his father in connection with a urinary misdeed. To this we will come in a moment. At any rate, the dreamer's shameful position is now entirely projected on another man, who seems old, weak, and in need of assistance.

The eliminative organ-mode has returned, as it were, from all the corridors and passages and rail lines, to its anatomical model and has overcome retention and delay: in the center of the visual field, a penis is micturating into a glass. The original body zone of dispute, that is the urethral organ, is now clearly seen ("in plastic form"), but alas it is the "old man's," while the dreamer is a benevolent helper, a sharp observer, and a cunning inventor. In fact, at this point in the dream (and there is such a point in a number of dreams reported by Freud), he feels particularly cunning because he is aware of discovering dream processes even as he dreamed. This is the point at which the dreamer awakes and becomes aware of his pressing need, having, we must note with awe, exerted an extraordinary dream effort to deny the need—and to secure for himself a new dream-specimen.

In reviewing the dream of Count Thun, I have endeavored to demonstrate that a configurational analysis substantiates the underlying themes to which the dreamer's association (omitted here) provide rich verbal access.

But it is time to record the childhood scenes "on whose account alone," as Freud says, "I embarked upon a discussion of this dream;" and it is incumbent on us to remember that this dream is part of a chapter on the importance of infantile material for the dream process.

"It appears," Freud reports, "that when I was two years old, I still occasionally wetted the bed, and when I was *reproached* [*Vorwürfe, vorhalten*] for this I consoled my father by promising to buy him a nice new red bed in N., the nearest town of any size. This was the origin of the parenthetical phrase in the dream to the effect that we had bought or had to buy the urinal in town: *one must keep one's promises.*

It will be seen how important was the word *"vorhalten"* ("hold against") in the description of the dreamer's solicitous service to the micturating old man. However, the scene also conveys the fact that the dreamer as a child warded off the shame by condescendingly consoling the father and by braggingly making a promise to him. A corresponding scene, at the age of seven or eight, is more serious, and (as the *Interpretation of Dreams* indicates) remained in Freud's memory as one of the most fateful scenes of his childhood.

When I was seven or eight years old there was another domestic scene, which I can remember very clearly. One evening before going to sleep I disregarded the rules which modesty lays down and obeyed the calls of nature in my parents' bedroom while they were present. In the course of his reprimand, my father let fall the words: *"The boy will come to nothing."* This must have been a frightful blow [*Kränkung*, insult] to my ambition, for references to this scene are still constantly recurring in my dreams and are always linked with an enumeration of my achievements and successes, as though I wanted to say: *"You see, I have come to something."*

The boy's delinquence—so one must specify in a changing technology—probably consisted of the use of a chamber-pot in his parents' bedroom. This crime, as well as the punishment by derisive shaming, and, most of all, the imperishable memory of the event, all point to a milieu in which such "character" weakness as the act of untimely and immodest urination becomes forcefully associated with the question of the boy's chances not only of ever becoming a man, but also of amounting to something, of becoming a "somebody": *was he promising,* or *did he promise too much?* In thus hitting the rebellious little exhibitionist in his weakest spot, the father not only followed his personal whim, but also the dictates of a certain culture area which tended to make youngsters defiantly ambitious (unless it succeeded in making them obediently submissive) by challenging them at significant times with the statement that they do not amount to much and with the prediction that they never will.

The two memories are thus connected by a theme of *ambition* which fits the whole context of this and other dreams reported by Freud: to promise something, to be promising, to promise much, to keep one's promise; or to promise too much —and to come to nothing.

What Freud wanted to demonstrate here we now take for granted, namely the method by which the reporter of a dream, in following his associations, can reconstruct the implicit lattice work which connects his adult dilemma with an infantile one and which, in fact, can lead to a significant childhood memory which then seems to have inspired the whole dream. We also understand the dominant wish-fulfillment in the dream: the shamed little boy's comeback, which also magically rights the man's grievance against the imperial authorities.

We, in turn, have reviewed the whole story in order to point out a dream's place within the study of a life history, and the systematic way in which a former stage of life, once it suggests itself for the process of dreaming, will reappear in an actuality which combines past and present: that is, the past insofar as it has remained actual in still calling for solutions and deeds (i.e., I keep what I promise); and the present insofar as its active tension remains vulnerable to past allusions of weakness or perdition.

What Freud first demonstrated in reporting this dream was the power of the infantile wish over the inner life of the adult. He did not take account of the alignment of the dream's wish-fulfillment with the actuality of the dreamer's total life space. But, as we can see, he did much more than most later workers can claim: he provided the data for further analysis.

Let me summarize, expanding what I have pointed out and

relating it to the associative material which came to Freud's mind after awakening. The *psychosexual stage* evoked is clear enough: beside the urethral zone and its function, the dream and especially the associations abound with references to "solid, liquid, and gaseous" excretions. What makes this dream extraordinary is the sweep and range of associations to the bodily emergency, the resiliency of "regressions," and the resourcefulness with which the dream locality and strategy is changed three times before it gives in to the waking power of the need. Thus the eliminative mode is transposed into all kinds of passageways, railroad lines, and exits—all "*besetzt.*" Through all of these the dreamer urgently needs to pass, escaping the attention of ticket collectors, examiners, and overeager female attendants. The physical "need to pass" urine is here translated from the cloacal body zone to major spatial configurations: the dreamer himself now "needs to pass" through disputed passages—a transfer from the autosphere to the macrosphere typically used in dreams and in play.

In the *psychosocial schedule* of development a trend toward *autonomy* and its counterpart, the sense of *shame*, coincide with the anal-urethral stage. I have also postulated the rudiments of *will* as the prime criterion of the ego strength of that same stage. All of this, too, seems to dominate Freud's urethral dream. The theme of autonomy combines the political allusions to the revolt of nationalist youth, to the rebellion of ethnic groups, to movements of provincial autonomy, and to wars of independence. Here *Autonomie* is obviously endowed with the affect of a personal need for impudent independence from the immodest relief of urinary needs in childhood to the insolent rebellion of the school boy, and from the "boorish" behavior of the college man to the megalomaniac thoughts of the vacation-bound doctor.

"Impudent" is in German *unverschämt*, that is, conspicuously lacking in the restraint imposed by a proper sense of shame. We see in the dream how the dreamer from this "over-compensatory" denial of embarrassment returns to the affect of shame. Correspondingly the problem of *will* arises in many forms: the willfulness of the infantile misdeed; the will power demanded of the little boy and the big traveler; the superior will of parents and authorities, and their own loss of self-control in incontinent senility; the will of authority and the unbroken will of the young; the nervous will of declining autocracy and the emerging will of the people. What impresses us here, then, is not only the developmental logic adhering to the complete inventory of images and attitudes of the stage perforce dominating the sleeper's actuality that night (urethral zone, eliminative-retentive mode, psychosocial autonomy, social shaming, and the problem of will) but, above all, the freedom with which the themes of this stage reach into all the co-ordinates of the adult man's actuality. For the dream of Count Thun also clearly points to the political trends in which the dreamer has found the closest affinity to his indomitably individualistic philosophy; and it ends, as I will now emphasize in conclusion, with a concomitant reaffirmation of the dreamer's phallic approach, his intellectual initiative and his professional identity.

As the old man is passing urine into the glass held before him, the dreamer is no longer a doomed little boy or a third-rate citizen, but (as he feels acutely) a benevolent healer, a sharp observer, and a cunning inventor. It cannot escape us that here the dreamer reacquires the true functions of his creative position in life; for he *is* a doctor inventing new methods, a liberator, and (in a professional context) a politician of the first order. In other words, he now exerts in the dream the kind of control which provides him with identity, competence, and power in his waking actuality; while those who would doubt him are pictured as old men who have lost control over their sphincters, over truth, and over him. His will is now autonomous and unlimited: "I thought of a plan . . . and then saw that this plan had already been put into effect. It was as if thinking and experiencing were one and the same thing."

This, then, is the culmination of a trend in the dream which Freud himself called megalomanic. It gave the dreamer a sense of cunning and a feeling of being able to escape "control at the exit." However, while the feeling tone of the dream may harbor a strong manic element, I will submit that it is the dream ego's duty to provide such self-engrandizement. For in view of every waking day's successive reminders of our unfulfilled and unfulfillable wishes, and of our lasting vulnerabilities and limitations, the dream must help us awake with a sense of wholeness, centrality, and competence—in other words, in an ego state of active tension. One could say—and I have said so in reviewing the Irma dream—that the dream must restore essential functions to their "conflict-free" state, although "absence of conflict" and "neutral energy" often seem somewhat miserly ways of characterizing our tie to actuality and to the world of deeds. Freud says that he knew as he dreamed that he understood dreams. The fact is that he *did* understand them better than any man before him when he was fully awake, and he was able to demonstrate what he knew in a great manner. And if, at the end of the dream, he takes care of the sad figure of an old man, he did, in life, take care not only of his dying father but of a growing host of previously misunderstood and incurable patients.

Dreams, then, besides obeying a *censor* who examines the onrushing wishes of the night, also appeal to a *sponsor* * who sanctions the sleeper's anticipation of activity, and may well be related to Roy Schafer's "loving super-ego." [17] I am reminded here of Bertram Lewin's lucid essay on Descartes' famous dream trilogy [18] which exerted the force of a revelation and is interpreted by Lewin both as an epileptic experience in sleep, and as "the place of origin" of the "Cartesian idea";

---

*This term was suggested by Dr. Kathleen Stewart.

and he wonders "what Einstein dreamt, or Leibnitz, or Lao-Tse." In relating a dream to a deed, I think Dr. Lewin and I would differ, as will become clear when I discuss historical actuality. Here, I would only point out that Descartes, also, had gone to bed in an agitated state "entirely taken up with the thought of having discovered the foundations of a science . . . marvellous." The ensuing dream, then, seems truly to represent a cataclysmic crisis: psychosomatic (for Descartes had been a sickly child); sexual (according to some vague allusions); moral (for there was the question whether God or the Devil had inspired his knowledge); and intellectual (was he right—and did he have the right to be right?). He was twenty-two then, and the dream trilogy appears to be a kind of private initiation rite permitting the young thinker to take his place in the history of thought. In his last dream there suddenly appears a man and behind him an unseen power which puts books and pictures before Descartes and makes them disappear again—clearly the power "that giveth and taketh away." Thus "sponsored," Descartes, too, decides in his dream that he knows he is dreaming and knows what the dream means.

At the end of Freud's dream of Count Thun, there is also an unknown man seemingly a victim of the ambitious dreamer's wish to escape infantile shame and to prove that he *is* "somebody." According to the translation, the man was blind even as the clever dreamer tries to make himself inconspicuous. In the original German, however, the man only *"stellte sich blind,"* i.e., he pretended to be blind, and this only in one eye. As an ocular gesture, this is reminiscent of the German phrase *"er drückte ein Auge zu,"* that is he "closed one eye," which means that he knew what was going on but let it pass. This gesture, in turn, is akin to winking; does it betray a fatherly conspiracy with the creative dreamer's "manic" self-confidence?

To conclude: Good sleep, by contract with the community, permits us to relax the safeguards of wakefulness and to recapitulate some past events. Dream life weaves the most recent dangers to the ego's sense of mastery into the tapestry of previous and distant ones, using personal delusion and private cunning to make one meaningfully patterned past of them all and to bring this past into line with anticipated actuality. As long as the sleeper can thus relax, dream well, and wake ready for action, do we really have a right to say that his ego in the state of sleep was "weak"? Has he not made such use of actuality as only an unregressed ego can make? A truly inactivated ego fails not only in dreaming, but also in awakening and, indeed, in being awake. If dreaming contains disguised fulfillments of infantile wishes, and if such wishes are thus prevented from disturbing sleep, there is ample reason to assume that good sleep and effective dreaming are necessary conditions for the nightly restoration of the ego's active tension. The dream, it is true, employs the most idiosyncratic means to review what is most personal, that is, psychic reality, but it also restores to the awakening sleeper the most effective means of sharing his actuality with those who share theirs with him.

This review of the dream of Count Thun has been undertaken with the double purpose of illustrating the ego's recovery of active tension through dreaming, and also of following the dream more systematically to the infantile stage of development re-actualized by the dream stimulus.. If we consider the dream of Count Thun predominantly eliminative, we cannot overlook the fact that urethral material also naturally presents phallic-urethral allusions; and one could go further and demonstrate that such allusions are accompanied by suggestions of another set of developmental data: the intrusive mode, initiative, guilt (or the denial of it), purpose—and some hysterical mechanisms. However, if we were to wish to review a whole dream specimen illustrating the actuality of the *third*, the *infantile-genital* stage of psychosexual development, I submit that Freud's dream of his patient Irma [19] is such a dream. But having reviewed this dream on a previous occasion,[20] I would like to go on to a subject which in the dream of Count Thun was prominent in the background only, namely, historical actuality.

WHAT A GOOD DREAMER can do for himself, psychoanalysis must restore to the patient: a productive interplay between psychological reality and historical actuality. Freud made a co-worker of each patient in the attempt to recover active ego tension by means of the psychoanalytic process. He turned free association, that meditative activity between dreaming and thinking, into a tool of study, but not without creating "the psychoanalytic situation"—an actuality of planfully restrained locomotion and minimal conventional interaction. Such an actuality, however, by arresting time as well as motion in the study à deux of unconscious processes and inner-dynamic changes, imparts a sense of historical process which can be in sharp contrast to the tempo of contemporary events. I would like, therefore, to say a word about psychoanalysis and historical actuality. We have used the dream of Count Thun to illustrate the way in which historical trends, participated in throughout a lifetime, reverberate in the adaptive processes observable in a man's dream. Our long-range objective is a better understanding of the interplay of inner life and actuality in men (leaders and followers) who together make history. Here one could, indeed, relate Freud's own life (and dream life) more systematically to the role which he eventually assumed in the history of ideas. However, I will now turn to methodological problems and to a variety of historical processes which will inevitably become our joint future concern.

History is as yet a relatively neglected field in psychoanalysis, although psychoanalysts have turned to *past history* to test their tools of reconstruction. But we can no longer abide by the one-way proposition which explains the behavior of leaders and of masses on the basis of the childhoods they had or had shared. In *Young Man Luther* [21] I used Luther's childhood and youth to show that a reformer and his childhood and the to-be-reformed and their childhoods, as well as the political actuality which brings them together in one decisive historical deed, are all aspects of an epoch's style of adaptation and re-adaptation.

There is a big step, then, from the clinic to history, a step not diminished in size and complexity by considering history a gigantic psychiatric hospital. In saying this, I paraphrase the statement of a drama critic in London who not long ago took a look around the London stage and exclaimed that history had become the dramatist's mental ward. He referred to plays which put such historical figures as T. E. Lawrence and Martin Luther on the stage, depicting both as almost too plausible mental patients and neither as the inspiring and effective man of action which he was in historical actuality, each, to be sure, for a limited period, bounded by neurotic suffering and historical tragedy.

The study of one man called great at first throws light primarily on other men in the same category. At MIT and at Harvard, we have studied other reformers and ideological innovators. Basic to their zeal (we found) is an infantile "account to settle," or what they themselves often refer to as a "curse" to be lived with, or to be lived down. Men like Luther, Gandhi, or Kierkegaard are not at all hesitant in specifying their respective curses in their diaries or public pronouncements. In Luther, for example, the curse was paternal brutality, whether it came from his father and his teachers, or from Rome and the Dogma as he perceived it as a child; in Gandhi, it was his father's death or rather his conviction that he let his father down on this final as well as on other occasions; in Kierkegaard, it was a strange curse connecting his own doom with that of his father's secret depravity. In each case, however, the fathers had tied their sons to themselves in such a way that overt rebellion or hate was impossible. By the same token, they had also imposed on their sons a sense of being both needed and chosen by their fathers, and thus of carrying a superior destiny and duty, although these very sons as children or youths felt isolated or weak, physically inferior or shy and cowardly. With proper safeguards one can go beyond these examples and find analogous themes: certainly Wilson will come to mind here and Eleanor Roosevelt, also a great innovator in the domain of women in public affairs. Such men and women have also in common an extraordinarily strong and precocious conscience in childhood, and have usually looked old in early years. They are given both to an excessive sense of unworthiness, and a precocious attention to "ultimate concerns." This they may try to throw off in youth by conventional and worldly means: Luther sang, Gandhi waltzed, and Kierkegaard drank—all for brief and disastrous periods. But then their early sense of being chosen settles in a conviction that in the conduct of their individual lives they carry the responsibility for a segment of mankind, if not for all existence, and they undergo their "great renunciation" which in turn frees them for being (as Wilson put it) "in love with activities on a large scale."

Much of what I have said so far, however, could be true also of a crank, or worse. One must add, therefore, that such men and women also display an unusual energy of body, a rare concentration of mind, and a total devotion of soul, which carries them through trials and errors and near catastrophes, and, above all, helps them to bide their time, until they find their public even as their public finds and drafts them.

It is at this nexus that some such theory as the psychosocial concept of identity becomes an historical tool. I will not repeat here its dynamic ingredients, as a conscious "sense" and yet also a deeply unconscious aspect of the person. Within historical actuality it is the sum of all images, ideas and forces which —roughly speaking—make a person (and a people) feel more "like themselves" and act more "like themselves,"—which means in historical terms: like what they have come to con-

sider their historical selves. By the same token, identity confusion defines what will make individuals and peoples feel that
they are betraying their core and losing their grip on "their"
times.

There are periods in history which are identity-vacua, when
a sudden sense of alienation is widespread. Our time shares with
Luther's an alienation composed of corresponding elements:
fears aroused by discoveries and inventions (including weapons) radically expanding and changing the space-time quality
of the world image; inner *anxieties* aggravated by the decay
of existing institutions which have provided the historical
anchor of an elite's identity; and the *dread* of an existential
vacuum. It is in such periods that the leaders' deep conflicts
and special gifts have found their "activities on a large scale,"
and that they have been found and chosen by contemporaries
possessed of analogous conflicts and corresponding needs. In
my study of Luther I endeavored to point out in some detail
how his lectures on the Psalms simultaneously reveal a self-
cure, a victorious if delayed formation of individual identity,
and also the promise to his countrymen of a rededicated Christian identity, rooted in Paulinian theology and yet "jointed"
to the political, technological and economic developments of
his day.

It belongs to the characteristics of a severe identity crisis,
however, that it vastly increases the need to delineate what one
is not, and to repudiate what is felt to be a foreign danger to
one's identity. Here, the human inability to overcome a certain
tribal and ideological territoriality becomes not only an obstacle to adaptation to changing events, but also a cause for
stampede and massacre.

It is obvious that psychoanalysis understands hot wars better
than cold ones; and that in the search for a possible leverage of
the psychoanalytic approach to history we have selected men
for study who select themselves by offering a wealth of passionate introspective data in diaries and in confessions and

whose historical actuality is defined by "hot" spiritual and ideological conflicts. One might say that by focusing on men strongly motivated by a sense of revelation (as, in a sense, even Wilson was) we have disqualified our approach from the analysis of decision makers who must keep a sense of personal revelation to a minimum and who cultivate cold and objective judgment, disciplined teamwork, and all the indices and safeguards of advanced technology. On closer study, however, revelation and historical decision (insofar as it remains an individual's decision) may prove to exist on the same continuum, namely, that of resolutions which will cause a sudden and irreversible shift in the destinies of leaders and led. For historical actuality is the attempt to create a future order out of the disorder of the past. The big historical decisions are simply those by which a leader or a leading group, being motivated and chosen to be in the lead, and possessing superior gifts of leadership, create a joint future out of a combination of their own pasts and the typical pasts of the led, and thus acquire and provide a conception of truth in action.

Truth in action, however, immediately redefines actuality, and thus takes immense chances. Gandhi once said (I quote from memory), "I am told that politics and religion belong to two different spheres. But I would say without a moment's hesitation and in all humility that those who say this do not know what religion is." But then came the terrible religious riots which besmirched the principle of non-violence with sadistic mob-rule on an unprecedented scale. Was Gandhi's influence a force comparable to that inherent in the rarest moments of charismatic revelation only, and was what followed him a colossal accident attributable to human frailty? Gandhi himself would never have accepted this verdict as, indeed, his dedication to both religion and politics forbade him to, wherefore he fasted when his followers failed him. Maybe it is time to study political sequences as psychological continuities rather than as accidental fatalities. In doing so, we would only extend to history—but extend with historical tools—an approach applied by Freud first to the neurotic accidents of life which, before him, were also considered mere fragmentations without coherent meaning.

The psychoanalyst's experience is that of studying, in case after case, the way in which a patient's integrative forces are inactivated by fragments of a past which impose themselves on actuality and yet refuse to be transformed into a future—fragments such as undigested memories, unsatisfied drives, unallayed fears, unconsummated relationships, unappeasable demands of conscience, unused capacities, incomplete patterns of identity, suppressed spiritual needs. By studying (in case histories, life histories, and biographies) those stages and crises of individual development in which the worst blockages of untransformable past seem to occur, the psychoanalyst in more recent years has also learned to discern the mechanisms, both individual and social, by which inner order is reactivated and renewed.

I feel, then, that one of the potential contributions of psychoanalysis to the study of historical processes could be the clarification of rigid and unconscious inner obstacles, stemming from past history, which obstruct emerging (and already strongly desired) decisions in present history. It could contribute to the delineation of what we may call *psycho-historical actuality*, that is, the sum of historical facts and forces which are of immediate relevance to the adaptive anticipations and to the mal-adaptive apprehensions in the individuals involved. Such inner-psychic relevance pervasively contributes to the prevalent sense of historical space-time in a given population. And what becomes most relevant to individuals as they live their individual life-histories will also determine their influence on future history. For historical actuality also points to the available resources which permit transformation of the past into a future of more inclusive identities.

A historical decision, however, is really a very condensed

moment in historical actuality, for here the resources of the maker of the decision and of those who must accept and sustain it fuse in one instant. To understand this, historians *and* psycho-analysts must learn to grasp fully the fact that while each individual life has its longitudinal logic, all lives lived inter-dependently within a given historical period share a kind of historical logic—and a-logic. Much of this is contained in the way and in the images by means of which men identify with each other, identify themselves with their institutions and their institutions with themselves, identify themselves with their leaders and their leaders with themselves, and how, as they thus identify, they repudiate (one might say dis-identify themselves from) their adversaries and enemies.

All of this has its antecedents in childhood and in identifica-tions with the first counterplayers in individual life. Every new beginning in later life, and every new attachment and involve-ment reverberates in the childhood strata of our images and our affects where all kings and leaders are fathers or big broth-ers and all countries and ideas, mothers. This we must learn both to take for granted and to subject to renewed study, for each age develops its own form of such interplay. What re-verberates in many persons at the same time, however, has a different quality from responses observable in isolated individ-uals. It differs, above all, in that closeness to concerted action which is decisive for its political significance.

Because nations and persons are entirely different systems, then, every infantile or pre-rational item thus recognized and named must be studied in its double nature of being a property of each individual life cycle, *and* of being a property of a communality, and for this reason subject to the fate of institu-tions. Psycho-historical actuality would therefore have two components: the relevance of historical changes for the iden-tity formation of the individual, and the relevance for further historical change of the kinds of identity formation which have become dominant in a given society in a given period of history.

A true leader, in turn, is obviously defined by his intuitive grasp of the actualities of the led, that is, of their readiness to act resourcefully in certain directions, and his ability to introduce himself into that actuality as a new, vital factor (personality, image, style). The success of any major decision made by him hinges on these two abilities. In trying to assess his position, then, we must know the actualities he deals with, as well as the influences which, at a given time, are acutely relevant for his followers' ability to accept a decision. For we know that a decision must mobilize given inner resources, and that a weakness in such mobilization leads to a large scale loss of identity and an inactivation of adaptive mechanisms which, in turn, unleashes (in groups as well as in individuals) irrational rages waiting only for the "first shot."

To acknowledge the power of these issues in psycho-historical actuality would mean to try to understand, at a given time, not only at what points individuals distort reality and threaten to regress with a vengeance, but also how ready they are in their actuality to transcend the remnants of the past, and to mobilize and cultivate more rational outlooks for the sake of a wider and more inclusive identification among men —such identification as provides the leverage for decisive deeds.

HEINZ HARTMANN has recently spoken of hidden preachers in our midst.[22] But if I have already taken advantage of the tradition which makes Sunday morning a suitable time for not-so-hidden preaching, I have at least abstained from the preacher's prerogative of recommending his text by associating it with possible catastrophes. Theories do not become truer by being made to fit emergencies, and there are dangers of a magnitude which forbids their being drawn into hasty theoretical controversy. But neither is it possible to ignore a shift in historical conditions which gives us a chilling sense of conceptual unpreparedness. At the end of the First World War, Freud could express the hope that after the carnage Eros would reassert its healing and reconciling power. Today it would be a fatally poisoned Eros trailing catastrophe.

Knowing this, some of us become strong partisans, as is anybody's birthright and duty when he feels his moment of participation in concerted action has arrived. We are concerned here only with the use of psychoanalytic concepts in dealing with political actuality. Here, most of us feel inhibited not only by the apathy we may share with other professions, but also by our special insights into human nature. For the conditions under which inner dynamics can be analyzed seem almost diametrically opposed to those under which political decisions can be made or influenced—opposed, that is, in the relative ratios of observation and action, and of introspection and resolution. To see this may be the first step in finding access to *ongoing history*.

We are often told that practitioners listening to life-histories for countless hours should be able to form an opinion about the influence of historical change on individuals. We wonder about this ourselves when, shaken by ominous turns in world events, we listen to our reclining customers associating "freely" and facing psychic reality staunchly, as they circumnavigate the concerns of the world community. Nor are we blind to the fact that only a limited number of patients or students after years of habituation to the psychoanalytic situation return to their actuality with a reinforced sense of familiarity. Not a few appear to be rather burdened and promptly undertake to burden home and work, profession and citizenship with the compulsion to superimpose psychic reality on shared actuality. In dealing with political change they insist on spreading this sense of reality over the social scene, unmasking disguises, exposing defenses and combating denials, and this with little consideration for the structure of public affairs. This tendency originates, of course, in the ethos of enlightenment which in psychoanalysis has found a new tool—and a new weapon. And since the psychoanalyst's professional identity is by its tradition and nature allied with the doctrines of rational enlightenment and personal freedom, he reinforces (as he finds himself reinforced by) those methods and weapons of liberalism which share a relative over-estimation of the value of mere awareness of "reality" and a neglect of the nature of political leverage.

Let me conclude, then, with a few remarks on the psychoanalytic method in relation to ongoing history. As indicated, we should grant from the outset that the actuality within which the psychoanalytic method may change a man is about as far removed from the making and sustaining of political decision as any two human situations could be. Psychoanalysis as a clinical method has a built-in governor which prevents both patient and analyst from entertaining decisive changes without having had time for sufficient retro- and introspection so that interpretation, anticipation, and prediction may all be based on extensive and proven post-diction. Psychoanalysis thus "works" only in a controlled setting where it serves the removal of neurotic hindrances, the reinstatement of nature that heals, and perhaps the freeing of genius that knows how to decide. I have indicated in what way I believe the psychoanalytic method might be applied to an understanding of massive resistances in whole populations to a change which they already desire and for which they are nearly ready. The decision itself, however, which will actualize such historical readiness must be a total response to the superior demand of "the hour," encompassing unconscious and conscious elements, personal and collective responses in a singular co-ordination. Psychological pre-occupation as such has little positive effect on and sometimes is even damaging to political or organizational judgment, as we know very well, for example, from the difficulties we encounter in our first attempts to organize psychoanalytic training under conditions vastly different from the days when we were proud to work underground—in every sense of the word. We, too, now have a history, as an organization and as a factor in Western culture; and it should not surprise us that we come to face the problem of our own history at a time when we—along with other humanists—come to study historical processes. New ideas, new movements, new countries, all act at first as if they were superseding history. To have a history, however, means to be heir to tragic guilt as well as to past error. Our earliest formulations of infantile sexuality, for example, have entered the sexual mores and the artistic imagery, not to speak of the self-conscious vocabulary, of our time in ways which we may well wish to disavow; and we have had and still have our share of id-utopias in which history is to be superseded by the power of infantile sexuality.

We cannot escape, then, the major task of our time—a task which we have helped to shape—namely, that of participating in historical actuality more consciously and thus responsibly than have the generations before us. But this is a problem at once methodological in its nature and ethical in its implications —as have, indeed, been all the problems on which psychoanalysis has focused. As always, then, only a clarification of our own position as observers and participants can (if anything will) guard the long range influence of our method. This consideration immediately leads to a few obvious caveats.

Even where and especially when his partisanship is clear, the psychoanalyst cannot use his method to debunk or to attack whom or what he abhors, but must apply the same measuring rod and the same assumption of a possible irrational or pathological involvement to the observer as well as to the observed; to the healer as well as to the sick; to the peace-seeker as well as to the warmonger, the thinker as well as the doer. Such universal objectivity, paired with enlightened partisanship, seems to me to be almost something of a psychoanalytic counterpart to the Hippocratic oath in medicine. Our method is, at any rate, so intrinsically humanistic that it can be effectively used only for continued enlightenment on a universal level and cannot become anybody's technique of subversion.

But if self-analysis is always an intrinsic part of the psycho-analytic method, then, I submit, we have not done our job in a respect essential to the understanding of history, that is in clarifying the relationship of our work to aggressive and de-structive action. It is not unusual, for example, to hear the "death-instinct" mentioned in interdisciplinary discussion as our principal explanation both for war-mindedness and for the paralysis of the peace-loving.

The fact that Freud, in his attempt to conceptualize death, preferred to remain within his "mythology" of instincts, and to speak of a "death-instinct," is a matter of the history of con-cept-formation. As such it has led many a psychoanalytic dis-cussion of open or covert destructiveness into speculative dead ends. Before disposing of Freud's ideas, however, one should always acknowledge that their grandeur at least suggested the immensity of the problem to be comprehended. Instead, how-ever, clinical observation has been further obscured by the ubiquitous term "aggression" which can mean anything from a determined approach to an object, to an attack with intent to annihilate. But I think that there is a more "actual" reason for the fact that man's ruthless striving for competence, mas-tery, and power has come under psychoanalytic scrutiny only gradually: I mean the understandable reluctance to recognize it in one's professional actuality. Activities of curing, under-standing, and theorizing are viewed with a suspicion of hidden sadism only if knives are used, living creatures dissected, or weapons refined. Yet, the history of psychoanalysis makes it clear that, like any investigative method, it can serve the drive for power and the need for a sharp if seemingly unbloody weapon. In this time of a tragic confrontation of "selfless" and "objective science" with its murderous results, however, it may well be up to psychoanalysis to initiate a self-scrutiny of the scientific mind.

That science can be used deliberately to aggravate warfare is clear, and modern scientific militarism has received much horrified attention. But contemporary history should make it clear that the matter of war and peace can no longer be considered one of the trigger-happiness of the war-minded on the one hand, and the peaceful pursuit of science and scholarship on the other. Was the role of science in the creation of nuclear armaments a natural outgrowth of technological progress paired with laudable national commitment and democratic sentiment? And was the subsequent escalation of competitive armaments an unnatural development resulting from the blind ambitions and apprehensions of men less "sane"? The intellectual observer and partisan, it seems, often refuses to face the historical role of men of the mind in the cycles of technical invention and wholesale destruction, of spiritual rejuvenation and moral fanaticism, of mutual understanding and righteous annihilation.

Robert Oppenheimer used the word "sin" for the scientist's sense of awakening to the danger which has befallen the whole human species. But does such tragic sin adhere to science only when scientists invent worse weapons than they meant to, and find them turned on targets not premeditated? Sin may be at any rate the wrong word. But there is something blind and boundless in the adventurous schemes of science and technology, which must now be understood in its historical and psychological relation to other modes of conquest and mastery, understood in its individual motivation and in its corporate development.

This, however, presupposes another restraint on some of our private and public arguments. Being preoccupied with the reality that cures, we also are apt to diagnose as irrational, and, therefore, sick or even "insane," pre-rational or a-rational modes of thinking such as characterize people in action. The analogy between individual insanity and mass irrationality, however, can be utterly misleading without a clarification of the systematic differences between the inner state of insane individuals and the social conditions conducive to mass irrationality. The question is, in fact, how irrationality persists along with pre-rational and rational thought processes, and this exactly in the sanest people and in the "right" institutions; for it is this combination which is apt to inactivate the adaptability, and blur the reason of the most calculating. Pre-rational mechanisms (such as projection and introjection) are developmentally early, structurally primitive, and yet basically necessary mechanisms of thought; and man (sane man) falls back on them not only in a state of irrationality, but also when lacking the information or the motivation for more rational thinking, and especially when possessed of that vague rage which accompanies a situation of *adaptive impotence*. The very fact that such rage, when exploited by leaders, may also be harnessed by them to superior standards of duty and performance indicates that such unreason is not of the nature of insanity. Its only cure is, in fact, a leadership which is competent in the use of political communication and yet also enlightened enough to avoid—for its own good—the glib exploitation of non-rational thinking.

To summarize: the psychoanalyst's way of looking at things permits him to detect in history those symptoms which reveal the deadening influence of the past on what could be a living future, and to discern indications of a more inclusive identity in the very core of hostile tensions. If this way of dealing with historical data, however, is to be applied to contemporary history, it needs a corresponding effort on the part of political historians and historically-minded politicians to separate out what, in the processes most familiar to them, they clearly recognize as traditional "complexes" prejudging ongoing history. In fragmentary and agitated form such efforts are all around us; a mature example would be George Kennan's book *Russia and the West under Lenin and Stalin*, which spells out a matter which he himself clearly considers to be on the borderline of psychology and politics, namely, the dangerous need on the part of his countrymen to see a defeated enemy surrender unconditionally—a need which has contributed significantly to the international tensions under which we live now. The question is whether historian and psychoanalyst can bridge the gap between psychic reality and historical actuality and discern together, not only whether and why a leader's or a people's opinions and actions seem irrational from a rationalist's point of view, but also what alternatives are most acute in historical actuality; not only what apprehensions seem to endanger, but also what opportunities seem to promise a more inclusive sense of identity and security. For collective as well as individual adaptation is furthered only by the proper ratio of insight offered and of action "sponsored."

I have now indicated (as far as I can discern it) the place of what I have called actuality both in the life-history and in history. The epistemologists among you have, no doubt, come to the conclusion that "reality" has always embodied what I have ascribed here to actuality. But I hope not to have taken up your time in vain by urging that it be included more deliberately and more systematically, in order to fill a gap in our understanding of historical as well as of infantile man.

VI

The Golden Rule in the Light of New Insight

One cannot long consider
the responsibilities suggested by new insight without
intruding on the domain of ethics. I was first encouraged to do so when asked to give the George W. Gay
Lecture on Medical Ethics in the Harvard Medical
School. The themes then presented are repeated and
elaborated in the following and final address which
was given for the University of Delhi and the India
International Centre in New Delhi in January 1963.

WHEN A LECTURE is announced one does not usually expect
the title to foretell very much about the content. But it must
be rare, indeed, that a title is as opaque as the one on your
invitation to this lecture: for it does not specify the field from
which new insight is to come and throw new light on the old
principle of the Golden Rule. You took a chance, then, in
coming, and now that I have been introduced as a psychoanalyst, you must feel that you have taken a double chance.

Let me tell you, therefore, how I came upon our subject.
In Harvard College, I teach a course, "The Human Life
Cycle." There (since I am by experience primarily a clinician)
we begin by considering those aggravated *crises* which mark
each stage of life and are known to psychiatry as potentially
pathogenic. But we proceed to discuss the potential *strengths*
which each stage contributes to human maturity. In either case,
so psychiatric experience and the observation of healthy children tell us, much depends on the interplay of generations in
which human strength can be revitalized or human weakness

219

perseverated "into the second and third generation." But this leads us to the role of the individual in the sequence of generations, and thus to that evolved order which your scriptures call *Lokasangraha*—the "maintenance of the world" (in Professor Radhakrishnan's translation). Through the study of case-histories and of life-histories we psychoanalysts have begun to discern certain fateful and certain fruitful patterns of interaction in those most concrete categories (parent and child, man and woman, teacher and pupil) which carry the burden of maintenance from generation to generation. The implication of our insights for ethics had preoccupied me before I came here; and, as you will well understand, a few months of animated discussion in India have by no means disabused me from such concerns. I have, therefore, chosen to tell you where I stand in my teaching, in the hope of learning more from you in further discussion.

My base line is the Golden Rule, which advocates that one should do (or not do) to another what one wishes to be (or not to be) done by. Systematic students of ethics often indicate a certain disdain for this all-too-primitive ancestor of more logical principles; and Bernard Shaw found the rule an easy target: don't do to another what you would like to be done by, he warned, because his tastes may differ from yours. Yet this rule has marked a mysterious meeting ground between ancient peoples separated by oceans and eras, and has provided a hidden theme in the most memorable sayings of many thinkers.

The Golden Rule obviously concerns itself with one of the very basic paradoxes of human existence. Each man calls his own a separate body, a self-conscious individuality, a personal awareness of the cosmos, and a certain death; and yet he shares this world as a *reality* also perceived and judged by others and as an *actuality* within which he must commit himself to ceaseless interaction. This is acknowledged in your scriptures as the principle of Karma.

To identify self-interest and the interest of other selves, the

Rule alternately employs the method of warning, "Do *not* as you would *not* be done by," and of exhortation, "Do, as you *would* be done by." For psychological appeal, some versions rely on a minimum of *egotistic prudence*, while others demand a maximum of *altruistic sympathy*. It must be admitted that the formula, "Do not to others what if done to you would cause you pain," does not presuppose much more than the mental level of the small child who desists from pinching when it gets pinched in return. More mature insight is assumed in the saying, "No one is a believer until he loves for his brother what he loves for himself." Of all the versions, however, none commit us as unconditionally as the Upanishad's, "he who sees all beings in his own self and his own self in all beings," and the Christian injunction, "love thy neighbor as thyself." They even suggest a true love and a true knowledge of ourselves. Freud, of course, took this Christian maxim deftly apart as altogether illusory, thus denying with the irony of the enlightenment what a maxim really is—and what (as I hope to show) his method may really stand for.

I will not (I could not) trace the versions of the Rule to various world religions. No doubt in English translation all of them have become somewhat assimilated to Biblical versions. Yet the basic formula seems to be universal, and it re-appears in an astonishing number of the most revered sayings of our civilization, from St. Francis' prayer to Kant's moral imperative and Lincoln's simple political creed: "As I would not be slave, I would not be master."

The variations of the Rule have, of course, provided material for many a discussion of ethics weighing the soundness of the logic implied and measuring the degree of ethical nobility reached in each. My field of inquiry, the clinical study of the human life cycle, suggests that I desist from arguing logical merit or spiritual worth and instead distinguish *variations in moral and ethical sensitivity* in accordance with stages in the development of human conscience.

The dictionary, our first refuge from ambiguity, in this case only confounds it: morals and ethics are defined as synonyms *and* antonyms of each other. In other words, they are the same, with a difference—a difference which I intend to emphasize. For it is clear that he who knows what is legal or illegal and what is moral or immoral has not necessarily learned thereby what is ethical. Highly moralistic people can do unethical things, while an ethical man's involvement in immoral doings becomes by inner necessity an occasion for tragedy.

I would propose that we consider *moral rules* of conduct to be based on a fear of *threats* to be forestalled. These may be outer threats of abandonment, punishment and public exposure, or a threatening inner sense of guilt, of shame or of isolation. In either case, the rationale for obeying a rule may not be too clear; it is the threat that counts. In contrast, I would consider *ethical rules* to be based on *ideals* to be striven for with a high degree of rational assent and with a ready consent to a formulated good, a definition of perfection, and some promise of self-realization. This differentiation may not agree with all existing definitions, but it is substantiated by the observation of human development. Here, then, is my first proposition: the moral and the ethical sense are different in their psychological dynamics, because the moral sense develops on an earlier, more immature level. This does not mean that the moral sense could be skipped, as it were. On the contrary, all that exists layer upon layer in an adult's mind has developed step by step in the growing child's, and all the major steps in the comprehension of what is considered good behavior in one's cultural universe are—for better and for worse—related to different stages in individual maturation. But they are all necessary to one another.

The response to a moral tone of voice develops early, and many an adult is startled when inadvertently he makes an infant cry, because his voice has conveyed more disapproval than he intended to. Yet, the small child, so limited to the intensity of the moment, somehow must learn the boundaries marked by "don'ts." Here, cultures have a certain leeway in underscoring the goodness of one who does not transgress or the evilness of one who does. But the conclusion is unavoidable that children can be made to feel evil, and that adults continue to project evil on one another and on their children far beyond the verdict of rational judgment. Mark Twain once characterized man as "the animal that blushes."

Psychoanalytic observation first established the psychological basis of a fact which Eastern thinkers have always known, namely, that the radical division into good and bad can be *the* sickness of the mind. It has traced the moral scruples and excesses of the adult to the childhood stages in which guilt and shame are ready to be aroused and are easily exploited. It has named and studied the "super-ego" which hovers over the ego as the inner perpetuation of the child's subordination to the restraining will of his elders. The voice of the super-ego is not always cruel and derisive, but it is ever ready to become so whenever the precarious balance which we call a good conscience is upset, at which times the secret weapons of this inner governor are revealed: the brand of shame and the bite of conscience. We who deal with the consequences in individual neuroses and in collective irrationality must ask ourselves whether excessive guilt and excessive shame are "caused" or merely accentuated by the pressure of parental and communal methods, by the threat of loss of affection, of corporal punishment, of public shaming. Or are they by now a proclivity for self-alienation which has become a part—and, to some extent, a necessary part—of man's evolutionary heritage?

All we know for certain is that the moral proclivity in man does not develop without the establishment of some chronic self-doubt and some truly terrible—even if largely submerged —rage against anybody and anything that reinforces such doubt. The "lowest" in man is thus apt to reappear in the guise of the "highest." Irrational and pre-rational combinations of goodness, doubt, and rage can re-emerge in the adult in those malignant forms of righteousness and prejudice which we may call *moralism*. In the name of high moral principles all the vindictiveness of derision, of torture, and of mass extinction can be employed. One surely must come to the conclusion that the Golden Rule was meant to protect man not only against his enemy's open attacks, but also against his friend's righteousness.

LEST THIS VIEW, in spite of the evidence of history, seem too "clinical," we turn to the writings of the evolutionists who in the last few decades have joined psychoanalysis in recognizing the superego as an evolutionary fact—and danger. The *developmental* principle is thus joined by an *evolutionary* one. Waddington [1] even goes so far as to say that super-ego rigidity may be an overspecialization in the human race, like the excessive body armor of the late dinosaurs. In a less grandiose comparison he likens the super-ego to "the finicky adaptation of certain parasites which fits them to live only on one host animal." In recommending his book, *The Ethical Animal*, I must admit that his terminology contradicts mine. He calls the awakening of morality in childhood a proclivity for "ethicizing," whereas I would prefer to call it moralizing. As do many animal psychologists, he dwells on analogies between the very young child and the young animal instead of comparing, as I think we must, the young animal with the pre-adult human, including the adolescent.

In fact, I must introduce here an amendment to my first, my "developmental" proposition, for between the development in childhood of man's *moral* proclivity and that of his *ethical* powers in adulthood, adolescence intervenes when he perceives the universal good in *ideological* terms. The imagery of steps in development, of course, is useful only where it is to be suggested that one item precedes another in such a way that the earlier one is necessary to the later ones and that each later one is of a higher order.

This "epigenetic" principle, according to which the constituent parts of a ground plan develop during successive stages, will be immediately familiar to you. For in the traditional Hindu concept of the life cycle the four intrinsic goals of life (Dharma, the orders that define virtue; Artha, the powers of the actual; Kama, the joys of libidinal abandon; and Moksha, the peace of deliverance) come to their successive and mutual perfection during the four stages, the ashramas of the apprentice, the householder, the hermit, and the ascetic. These stages are divided from each other by sharp turns of direction; yet, each depends on the previous one, and whatever perfection is possible depends on them all.

I would not be able to discuss the relation of these two foursomes to each other, nor ready to compare this ideal conception to our epigenetic views of the life cycle. But the affinities of the two conceptions are apparent, and at least the ideological indoctrination of the apprentice, the Brahmacharya, and the ethical one of the Grihasta, the householder, correspond to the developmental categories suggested here.

No wonder; for it is the joint development of cognitive and emotional powers paired with appropriate social learning which enables the individual to realize the potentialities of a stage. Thus youth becomes ready—if often only after a severe bout with moralistic regression—to envisage the more universal principles of a highest human good. The adolescent learns to grasp the flux of time, to anticipate the future in a coherent way, to perceive ideas and to assent to ideals, to take—in short —an *ideological* position for which the younger child is cognitively not prepared. In adolescence, then, an ethical view is approximated, but it remains susceptible to an alternation of impulsive judgment and odd rationalization. It is, then, as true for adolescence as it is for childhood that man's way stations to maturity can become fixed, can become premature end stations, or stations for future regression.

The moral sense, in its perfections and its perversions, has been an intrinsic part of man's *evolution*, while the sense of ideological rejuvenation has pervaded his *revolutions*, both with prophetic idealism and with destructive fanaticism. Adolescent man, in all his sensitivity to the ideal, is easily exploited by promises of counterfeit millennia, easily taken in by the promise of a new and arrogantly exclusive identity.

The *true* ethical sense of the young adult, finally, encompasses and goes beyond moral restraint and ideal vision, while insisting on concrete commitments to those intimate relationships and work associations by which man can hope to share a lifetime of productivity and competence. But young adulthood engenders its own dangers. It adds to the moralist's righteousness, and to the ideologist's fanatic repudiation of all otherness, the *territorial defensiveness* of one who has appropriated and staked out his earthly claim and who seeks eternal security in the super-identity of organizations. Thus, what the Golden Rule at its highest has attempted to make all-inclusive, tribes and nations, castes and classes, moralities and ideologies have consistently made exclusive again—proudly, superstitiously, and viciously denying the status of reciprocal ethics to those "outside."

If I have so far underscored the malignant potentials of man's slow maturation, I have done so not in order to dwell on a kind of dogmatic pessimism which can emerge all too easily from clinical preoccupation and often leads only to anxious avoidances. I know that man's moral, ideological, and ethical propensities can find, and have found on occasion, a sublime integration, in individuals and in groups who were both tolerant and firm, both flexible and strong, both wise and obedient. Above all, men have always shown a dim knowledge of their better potentialities by paying homage to those purest leaders who taught the simplest and most inclusive rules for an undivided mankind. I will have a word to say later about Gandhi's continued "presence" in India. But men have also persistently betrayed them, on what passed for moral or ideological grounds, even as they are now preparing a potential betrayal of the human heritage on scientific and technological grounds in the name of that which is considered good merely because it can be made to work—no matter where it leads. No longer do we have license to emphasize either the "positive" or the "negative" in man. Step for step, they go together: moralism with moral obedience, fanaticism with ideological devotion, and rigid conservatism with adult ethics.

Man's socio-genetic evolution is about to reach a crisis in the full sense of the word, a crossroads offering one path to fatality, and one to recovery and further growth. Artful perverter of joy and keen exploiter of strength, man is the animal that has learned to survive "in a fashion," to multiply without food for the multitudes, to grow up healthily without reaching personal maturity, to live well but without purpose, to invent ingeniously without aim, and to kill grandiosely without need. But the processes of socio-genetic evolution also seem to promise a new humanism, the acceptance by man—as an evolved product as well as a producer, and a self-conscious tool of further evolution—of the obligation to be guided in his planned actions and his chosen self-restraints by his knowledge and his insights. In this endeavor, then, it may be of a certain importance to learn to understand and to master the differences between infantile morality, adolescent ideology and adult ethics. Each is necessary to the next, but each is effective only if they eventually combine in that wisdom which, as Waddington puts it, "fulfills sufficiently the function of mediating evolutionary advance."

At the point, however, when one is about to end an argument with a global injunction of what we *must* do, it is well to remember Blake's admonition that the common good readily becomes the topic of "the scoundrel, the hypocrite, and the flatterer;" and that he who would do some good must do so in "minute particulars." And indeed, I have so far spoken only of the developmental and the evolutionary principle, according to which the propensity for ethics grows in the individual as part of an adaptation roughly laid down by evolution. Yet, to grow in the individual, ethics must be generated and re-generated in and by the sequence of generations—again, a matter fully grasped and systematized, some will say stereo-typed, in the Hindu tradition. I must now make more explicit what our insights tell us about this process.

LET ME MAKE an altogether new start here. Let us look at sci-entific man in his dealings with animals and let us assume (this is not a strange assumption in India) that animals, too, may have a place close to the "other" included in the Rule. The psychologists among you know Professor Harry Harlow's studies on the development of what he calls affection in mon-keys.[2] He did some exquisite experimental and photographic work attempting, in the life of laboratory monkeys, to "con-trol the mother variable." He took monkeys from their mothers within a few hours after birth, isolated them and left them with "mothers" made out of wire, metal, wood, and terry cloth. A rubber nipple somewhere in their middles emitted piped-in milk, and the whole contraption was wired for body warmth. All the "variables" of this mother situation were controlled: the amount of rocking, the temperature of the "skin," and the exact incline of the maternal body necessary to make a scared monkey feel safe and comfortable. Years ago, when this method was presented as a study of the development of af-fection in monkeys, the clinician could not help wondering whether the small animals' obvious attachment to this con-traption was really *monkey* affection or a fetishist addiction to inanimate objects. And, indeed, while these laboratory reared monkeys became healthier and healthier, and much more easily trained in technical know-how than the inferior animals brought up by mere monkey mothers, they became at the end what Harlow calls "psychotics." They sit passively, they stare vacantly, and some do a terrifying thing: when poked they bite themselves and tear at their own flesh until the blood flows. They have not learned to experience "the other," whether as mother, mate, child—or enemy. Only a tiny minority of the females produced offspring, and only one of them made an attempt to nurse hers. But science remains a wonderful thing. Now that we have succeeded in producing "psychotic" monkeys experimentally, we can convince ourselves that we have at last given scientific support to the theory that severely disturbed mother-child relationships "cause" human psychosis.

This is a long story; but it speaks for Professor Harlow's methods that what they demonstrate is unforgettable. At the same time, they lead us to that borderline where we recognize that the scientific approach toward living beings must be with concepts and methods adequate to the study of ongoing life, not of selective extinction. I have put it this way: one can study the nature of things by doing something *to* them, but one can really learn something about the essential nature of living beings only by doing something *with* them or *for* them. This, of course, is the principle of clinical science. It does not deny that one can learn by dissecting the dead, or that animal or man can be motivated to lend circumscribed parts of themselves to an experimental procedure. But for the study of those central transactions which are the carriers of socio-genetic evolution, and for which we must take responsibility in the future, the chosen unit of observation must be the generation, not the individual. Whether an individual animal or human being has partaken of the stuff of life can only be tested by the kind of observation which includes his ability to transmit life—in some essential form—to the next generation.

One remembers here the work of Konrad Lorenz, and the

kind of "inter-living" research which he and others have developed, making—in principle—the life cycle of certain selected animals part of the same environment in which the observer lives his own life cycle, studying his own role as well as theirs and taking his chances with what his ingenuity can discern in a setting of sophisticated naturalist inquiry. One remembers also Elsa the Lioness, a foundling who was brought up in the Adamson household in Kenya. There the mother variable was not controlled, it was in control. Mrs. Adamson and her husband even felt responsible for putting grown-up Elsa back among the lions and succeeded in sending her back to the bush, where she mated and had cubs, and yet came back from time to time (accompanied by her cubs) to visit her human foster parents. In our context, we cannot fail to wonder about the built-in "moral" sense that made Elsa respond—and respond in very critical situations, indeed—to the words, "No, Elsa, no," *if* the words came from human beings she trusted. Yet, even with this built-in "moral" response, and with a lasting trust in her foster parents (which she transmitted to her wild cubs) she was able to live as a wild lion. Her mate, however, never appeared; he apparently was not too curious about her folks.

The point of this and similar stories is that our habitual relationship to what we call beasts in nature and "instinctive" or "instinctual" beastliness in ourselves may be highly distorted by thousands of years of superstition, and that there may be resources for peace even in our "animal nature" if we will only learn to nurture nature, as well as to master it. Today, we can teach a monkey, in the very words of the Bible, to "eat the flesh of his own arm," even as we can permit "erring leaders" to make of all mankind the "fuel of the fire." Yet, it seems equally plausible that we can also let our children grow up to lead "the calf and the young lion and the fatling together"— in nature and in their own nature.

To RECOGNIZE one of man's prime resources, however, we must trace back his individual development to his *pre-moral* days, his infancy. His earliest social experimentation at that time leads to a certain ratio of basic trust and basic mistrust—a ratio which, if favorable, establishes the fundamental human strength: hope. This over-all attitude emerges as the newborn organism reaches out to its caretakers and as they bring to it what we will now discuss as *mutuality*. The failure of basic trust and of mutuality has been recognized in psychiatry as the most far-reaching failure, undercutting all development. We know how tragic and deeply pathogenic its absence can be in children and parents who cannot arouse and cannot respond. It is my further proposition, then, that all moral, ideological, and ethical propensities depend on this early experience of mutuality.

I would call mutuality a relationship in which partners depend on each other for the development of their respective strengths. A baby's first responses can be seen as part of an actuality consisting of many details of mutual arousal and response. While the baby initially smiles at a mere configuration resembling the human face, the adult cannot help smiling back, filled with expectations of a "recognition" which he needs to secure from the new being as surely as it needs him. The fact is that the mutuality of adult and baby is the original source of hope, the basic ingredient of all effective as well as ethical human action. As far back as 1895, Freud, in his first outline of a "Psychology for Neurologists," confronts the "helpless" newborn infant with a "help-rich" ("*hilfreich*") adult, and postulates that their mutual understanding is "the primal source of all moral motives." [3] Should we, then, endow the Golden Rule with a principle of mutuality, replacing the reciprocity of both prudence and sympathy?

Here we must add the observation that a parent dealing with a child will be strengthened in *his* vitality, in *his* sense of identity, and in *his* readiness for ethical action by the very ministrations by means of which he secures to the child vitality, future identity, and eventual readiness for ethical action.

But we should avoid making a new Utopia out of the "mother-child relationship." The paradise of early childhood must be abandoned—a fact which man has as yet not learned to accept. The earliest mutuality is only a beginning and leads to more complicated encounters, as both the child and his interaction with a widening circle of persons grow more complicated. I need only point out that the second basic set of vital strengths in childhood (following trust and hope) is autonomy and will, and it must be clear that a situation in which the child's willfulness faces the adult's will is a different proposition from that of the mutuality of instilling hope. Yet, any adult who has managed to train a child's will must admit— for better or for worse—that he has learned much about himself and about will that he never knew before, something which cannot be learned in any other way. Thus each growing individual's developing strength "dovetails" with the strengths of an increasing number of persons arranged about him in the formalized orders of family, school, community and society. But orders and rules are kept alive only by those "virtues" of which Shakespeare says (in what appears to me to be *his* passionate version of the Rule) that they, "shining upon others heat them and they retort that heat again to the first giver."

One more proposition must be added to the developmental and to the generational one, and to that of mutuality. It is implied in the term "activate," and I would call it the principle of *active choice*. It is, I think, most venerably expressed in St. Francis's prayer: "Grant that I may not so much seek to be consoled as to console; to be understood, as to understand; to be loved as to love; for it is in giving that we receive." Such commitment to an initiative in love is, of course, contained in the admonition to "love thy neighbor." I think that we can recognize in these words a psychological verity, namely, that only he who approaches an encounter in a (consciously and unconsciously) active and giving attitude, rather than in a demanding and dependent one, will be able to make of that encounter what it can become.

WITH THESE CONSIDERATIONS in mind, then, I will try to formulate my understanding of the Golden Rule. I have been reluctant to come to this point; it has taken thousands of years and many linguistic acrobatics to translate this Rule from one era to another and from one language into another, and at best one can only confound it again, in a somewhat different way.

I would advocate a general orientation which has its center in whatever activity or activities gives man the feeling, as William James put it, of being "most deeply and intensely active and alive." In this, so James promises, each one will find his "real me"; but, I would now add, he will also acquire the experience that *truly worthwhile acts enhance a mutuality between the doer and the other—a mutuality which strengthens the doer even as it strengthens the other.* Thus, the "doer" and "the other" are partners in one deed. Seen in the light of human development, this means that the doer is activated in whatever strength is *appropriate to his age, stage, and condition,* even as he activates in the other the strength appropriate to *his* age, stage and condition. Understood this way, the Rule would say that it is best to do to another what will strengthen you even as it will strengthen him—that is, what will develop his best potentials even as it develops your own.

This variation of the Rule is obvious enough when applied to the relation of parent and child. But does the uniqueness of their respective positions, which has served as our model so far, have any significant analogies in other situations in which uniqueness depends on a divided function?

To return to particulars, I will attempt to apply my amendment to the diversity of function in the two sexes. I have not dwelled so far on this most usual subject of a psychoanalytic discourse, sexuality. So much of this otherwise absorbing aspect of life has, in recent years, become stereotyped in theoretical discussion. Among the terminological culprits to be blamed for this sorry fact is the psychoanalytic term "love object." For this word "object" in Freud's theory has been taken too literally by many of his friends and by most of his enemies—and moralistic critics do delight in misrepresenting a man's transitory formulations as his ultimate "values." The fact is that Freud, on purely conceptual grounds, and on the basis of the scientific language of his laboratory days, pointed out that drive energies have "objects." But he certainly never advocated that men or women should treat one another as objects on which to live out their sexual idiosyncrasies.

Instead, his central theory of genitality which combines strivings of sexuality and of love points to one of those basic mutualities in which *a partner's potency and potentialities are activated even as he activates the other's potency and potentialities.* Freud's theory implies that a man will be more a man to the extent to which he makes a woman more a woman—and vice versa—because only two uniquely different beings can enhance their respective uniqueness for one another. A "genital" person in Freud's sense is thus more apt to act in accordance with Kant's version of the Golden Rule, in that he would so act as to treat humanity "whether in his person or in another, always as an end, and never as only a means." What Freud added to the ethical principle, however, is a methodology which opens to our inquiry and to our influence the powerhouse of inner forces. For they provide the shining heat for our strengths—and the smoldering smoke of our weaknesses.

I cannot leave the subject of the two sexes without a word on the uniqueness of women. One may well question whether or not the Rule in its oldest form tacitly meant to include women as partners in the golden deal. Today's study of lives still leaves quite obscure the place of women in what is most relevant in the male image of man. True, women are being granted *equality* of political rights, and the recognition of a certain *sameness* in mental and moral equipment. But what they have not begun to earn, partially because they have not cared to ask for it, is the *equal right to be effectively unique,* and to use hard-won rights in the service of what they uniquely represent in human evolution. The West has much to learn, for example, from the unimpaired womanliness of India's modern women. But there is today a universal sense of the emergence of a new feminism as part of a more inclusive humanism. This coincides with a growing conviction—highly ambivalent, to be sure—that the future of mankind cannot depend on men alone and may well depend on the fate of a "mother variable" uncontrolled by technological man. The resistance to such a consideration always comes from men and women who are mortally afraid that by emphasizing what is unique one may tend to re-emphasize what is unequal. And, indeed, the study of life histories confirms a far-reaching sameness in men and women insofar as they express the mathematical architecture of the universe, the organization of logical thought, and the structure of language. But such a study also suggests that while boys and girls can think and act and talk alike, they naturally do not experience their bodies (and thus the world) alike. I have attempted to demonstrate this by pointing to sex differences in the structuralization of space in the play of children.[4] But I assume that a uniqueness of either sex will be granted without proof, and that the "difference" acclaimed by the much-quoted Frenchman is not considered only a matter of anatomical appointments for mutual sexual enjoyment, but a psychobiological difference central to two great modes of life, the *paternal* and the *maternal* modes. The amended Golden

Rule suggests that one sex enhances the uniqueness of the other; it also implies that each, to be really unique, depends on a mutuality with an equally unique partner.

FROM THE MOST intimate human encounters we now turn to a professional, and yet relatively intimate, one: that between healer and patient. There is a very real and specific inequality in the relationship of doctor and patient in their roles of knower and known, helper and sufferer, practitioner of life and victim of disease and death. For this reason medical people have their own and unique professional oath and strive to live up to a universal ideal of "the doctor." Yet the practice of the healing arts permits extreme types of practitioners, from the absolute authoritarian over homes and clinics to the harassed servant of demanding mankind, from the sadist of mere proficiency, to the effusive lover of all (well, almost all) of his patients. Here, too, Freud has thrown intimate and original light on the workings of a unique relationship. His letters to his friend and mentor Fliess illustrate the singular experience which made him recognize in his patients what he called "transference"—that is, the patient's wish to exploit sickness and treatment for infantile and regressive ends. But more, Freud, recognized a "countertransference" in the healer's motivation to exploit the patient's transference and to dominate or serve, possess or love him to the disadvantage of his true function. He made systematic insight into transference *and* countertransference part of the training of the psychoanalytic practitioner.

I would think that all of the motivations necessarily entering so vast and so intricate a field could be reconciled in a Golden Rule amended to include a mutuality of divided function. Each specialty and each technique in its own way permits the medical man to *develop as a practitioner, and as a person, even as the patient is cured as a patient, and as a person.* For a real cure transcends the transitory state of patienthood. It is an experience which enables the cured patient to develop and to transmit to home and neighborhood an attitude toward health which is one of the most essential ingredients of an ethical outlook.

Beyond this, can the healing arts and sciences contribute to a new ethical outlook? This question always recurs in psychoanalysis and is usually disposed of with Freud's original answer that the psychoanalyst represents the ethics of scientific truth only and is committed to studying ethics (or morality) in a scientific way. Beyond this, he leaves *Weltanschauungen* (ethical world views) to others.

It seems to me, however, that the clinical arts and sciences, while employing the scientific method, are not defined by it or limited by it. The healer is committed to a highest good, the preservation of life and the furtherance of well-being— the "maintenance of life." He need not prove scientifically that these are, in fact, the highest good; rather, he is precommitted to this basic proposition while investigating what can be verified by scientific means. This, I think, is the meaning of the Hippocratic oath, which subordinates all medical method to a humanist ethic. True, a man can separate his personal, his professional, and his scientific ethics, seeking fulfillment of idiosyncratic needs in personal life, the welfare of others in his profession, and truths independent of personal preference or service in his research. However, there are psychological limits to the multiplicity of values a man can live by, and, in the end, not only the practitioner, but also his patient and his research, depend on a certain unification in him of temperament, intellect, and ethics. This unification clearly characterizes great doctors.

While it is true, then, that as scientists we must study ethics objectively, we are, as professional individuals, committed to a unification of personality, training, and conviction which alone will help us to do our work adequately. At the same time, as transient members of the human race, we must record the truest meaning of which the fallible methods of our era and the accidental circumstances of our existence have made us aware. In this sense, there is (and always has been) not only an ethics governing clinical work, and a clinical approach to the study of ethics, but also a contribution to ethics of the healing orientation. The healer, furthermore, has now committed himself to prevention on a large scale, and he cannot evade the problem of assuring ethical vitality to all lives saved from undernourishment, morbidity, and early mortality. Man's technical ability and social resolve to prevent accidental conception makes every child conceived a subject of universal responsibility.

As I APPROACH my conclusion, let me again change my focus and devote a few minutes to a matter political and economic as well as ethical: Gandhi's "Rule."

In Ahmedabad I had occasion to visit Gandhi's ashram across the Sabarmati River; and it was not long before I realized that in Ahmedabad a hallowed and yet eminently concrete event had occured which perfectly exemplifies everything I am trying to say. I refer, of course, to Gandhi's leadership in the lock-out and strike of the mill-workers in 1918, and his first fast in a public cause. This event is well known in the history of industrial relations the world over, and vaguely known to all educated Indians. Yet, I believe that only in Ahmedabad, among surviving witnesses and living institutions, can one fathom the "presence" of that event as a lastingly successful "experiment" in local industrial relations, influential in Indian politics, and, above all, representing a new type of encounter in divided human functions. The details of the strike and of the settlement need not concern us here. As usual, it began as a matter of wages. Nor can I take time to indicate the limited political and economic applicability of the Ahmedabad experiment to other industrial areas in and beyond India. What interests us here, is the fact that Gandhi, from the moment of his entry into the struggle, considered it an occasion not for maximum reciprocal coercion resulting in the usual compromise, but as an opportunity for all—the workers, the owners, and himself—"to rise from the present conditions." [5]

The utopian quality of the principles on which he determined to focus can only be grasped by one who can visualize the squalor of the workmen's living conditions, the latent panic in the ranks of the paternalistic millowners (beset by worries of British competition), and Gandhi's then as yet relative experience in handling the masses of India. The shadows of defeat, violence and corruption hovered over every one of the "lofty" words which I am about to quote. But to Gandhi, any worthwhile struggle must "transform the inner life of the people." Gandhi spoke to the workers daily under the famous Babul Tree outside the medieval Shahpur Gate. He had studied their desperate condition, yet he urged them to ignore the threats and the promises of the millowners who in the obstinate fashion of all "haves" feared the anarchic insolence and violence of the "have nots." He knew that they feared him, too, for they had indicated that they might even accept his terms if only he would promise to leave and to stay away forever. But he settled down to prove that a just man could "secure the good of the workers while safeguarding the good of the employers"—the two opposing sides being represented by a sister and a brother, Anasuyabehn and Ambalal Sarabhai. Under the Babul Tree Gandhi announced the principle which somehow corresponds to our amended Rule: *"That line of action is alone justice which does not harm either party to a dispute."* By harm he meant—and his daily announcements leave no doubt of this—an inseparable combination of economic disadvantage, social indignity, loss of self-esteem, and latent vengeance.

Neither side found it easy to grasp this principle. When

the workers began to weaken, Gandhi suddenly declared a fast. Some of his friends, he admitted, considered this "foolish, unmanly, or worse"; and some were deeply distressed. But, "I wanted to show you," he said to the workers, "that I was not playing with you." He was, as we would say, in dead earnest, and this fact, then as later, immediately raised an issue of local conscience to national significance. In daily appeals, Gandhi stressed variously those basic inner strengths without which no issue has "virtue," namely, will with justice, purpose with discipline, respect for work of any kind, and truthfulness. But he knew, and he said so, that these masses of illiterate men and women, newly arrived from the villages and already exposed to proletarization, did not have the moral strength or the social solidarity to adhere to principle without strong leadership. "You have yet to learn how and when to take an oath," he told them. The oath, the dead earnestness, then, was as yet the leader's privilege and commitment. In the end the matter was settled, not without a few Gandhian compromises to save face all around, but with a true acceptance of the settlement originally proposed by Gandhi.

I do not claim to understand the complex motivations and curious turns of Gandhi's mind—some contradicting Western rigidity in matters of principle, and some, I assume, strange to Indian observers, as well. I can also see in Gandhi's actions a paternalism which may now be "dated." But his monumental simplicity and total involvement in the "experiment" made both workers and owners revere him. And he himself said with humorous awe, "I have never come across such a fight." For, indeed both sides had matured in a way that lifted labor relations in Ahmedabad to a new and lasting level. Let me quote only the fact that, in 1950, the Ahmedabad Textile Labor Organization accounted for only a twentieth of India's union membership, but for eighty per cent of its welfare expenditures.

Such a singular historical event, then, reveals something essential in human strength, in traditional Indian strength and in the power of Gandhi's own personal transformation at the time. To me, the miracle of the Ahmedabad experiment has been not only its lasting success and its tenacity during those days of anarchic violence which after the great partition broke down so many dams of solidarity, but above all, the spirit which points beyond the event.

AND NOW A FINAL WORD on what is, and will be for a long time to come, the sinister horizon of the world in which we all study and work: the international situation. Here, too, we cannot afford to live for long with a division of personal, professional, and political ethics—a division endangering the very life which our professions have vowed to keep intact, and thus cutting through the very fiber of our personal existence. Only in our time, and in our very generation, have we come, with traumatic suddenness, to be conscious of what was self-evident all along, namely, that in all of previous history the Rule, in whatever form, has comfortably coexisted with warfare. A warrior, all armored and spiked and set to do to another what he fully expected the other to be ready to do to him, saw no ethical contradiction between the Rule and his military ideology. He could, in fact, grant to his adversary a respect which he hoped to earn in return. This tenuous coexistence of ethics and warfare may outlive itself in our time. Even the military mind may well come to fear for its historical identity, as boundless slaughter replaces tactical warfare. What is there, even for a "fighting man" in the Golden Rule of the Nuclear Age, which seems to say, "Do not unto others—unless you are sure you can do them in as totally as they can do you in"?

One wonders, however, whether this deadlock in international morals can be broken by the most courageous protest, the most incisive interpretation, or the most prophetic warning—a warning of catastrophe so all-consuming that most men must ignore it, as they ignore their own death and have learned to ignore the monotonous prediction of hell. It seems, instead, that only an ethical orientation, a direction for vigorous co-operation, can free today's energies from their bondage in armed defensiveness. We live at a time in which—with all the species-wide destruction possible—we can think for the first time of a species-wide identity, of a truly universal ethics, such as has been prepared in the world religions, in humanism, and by some philosophers. Ethics, however, cannot be fabricated. They can only emerge from an informed and inspired search for a more inclusive human identity, which a new technology and a new world image make possible as well as mandatory. But again, all I can offer you here is another variation of the theme. What has been said about the relationships of parent and child, of man and woman, and of doctor and patient, may have some application to the relationship of nations to each other. Nations today are by definition units at different stages of political, technological and economic transformation. Under these conditions, it is all too easy for over-developed nations to believe that nations, too, should treat one another with a superior educative or clinical attitude. The point of what I have to say, however, is not underscored inequality, but respected unique-ness within historical differences. Insofar as a nation thinks of itself as a collective individual, then, it may well learn to visual-ize its task as that of maintaining mutuality in international relations. For the only alternative to armed competition seems to be the effort to *activate in the historical partner what will strengthen him in his historical development even as it strength-ens the actor in his own development—toward a common future identity.* Only thus can we find a common denominator in the rapid change of technology and history and transcend the dangerous imagery of victory and defeat, of subjugation and exploitation which is the heritage of a fragmented past.

Does this sound utopian? I think, on the contrary, that all of what I have said is already known in many ways, is being expressed in many languages, and practiced on many levels. At our historical moment it becomes clear in a most practical way that the doer of the Golden Rule, and he who is done by, is the same man, *is* man.

Men of clinical background, however, must not lose sight of a dimension which I have taken for granted here. While the Golden Rule in its classical versions prods man to strive *consciously* for a highest good and to avoid mutual harm with a sharpened awareness, our insights assume an *unconscious* substratum of ethical strength and, at the same time, unconscious arsenals of destructive rage. The last century has traumatically expanded man's awareness of unconscious motivations stemming from his animal ancestry, from his economic history, and from his inner estrangements. It has also created (in all these respects) methods of productive self-analysis. These I consider the pragmatic Western version of that universal trend toward self-scrutiny which once reached such heights in Asian tradition. It will be the task of the next generation everywhere to begin to integrate new and old methods of self-awareness with the minute particulars of universal technical proficiency.

It does not seem easy to speak of ethical subjects without indulging in some moralizing. As an antidote I will conclude with the Talmudic version of the Rule. Rabbi Hillel once was asked by an unbeliever to tell the whole of the Torah while he stood on one foot. I do not know whether he meant to answer the request or to remark on its condition when he said: "What is hateful to yourself, do not to your fellow man. That is the whole of the Torah and the rest is but commentary." At any rate, he did not add: "Act accordingly." He said: "Go, and learn it."

References

I The First Psychoanalyst

1. Ernest Jones, *The Life and Work of Sigmund Freud*, New York: Basic Books, 1953.
2. Sigmund Freud, "Fragment of an Analysis of a Case of Hysteria" [1905], *Standard Edition*, 7:3–122, London: Hogarth Press, 1953.
3. Sigmund Freud, *The Origins of Psychoanalysis: Letters to Wilhelm Fliess, Drafts and Notes: 1887–1902*, edited by Marie Bonaparte, Anna Freud and Ernst Kris, New York: Basic Books, 1954.
4. Sigmund Freud, *The Interpretation of Dreams* [1900], *Standard Edition*, 4, London: Hogarth Press, 1953.
5. David Rapaport, "The Structure of Psychoanalytic Theory: A Systemizing Attempt," in *Psychology: A Study of a Science*, Vol. III, edited by Sigmund Koch, New York: McGraw-Hill, 1959.

II The Nature of Clinical Evidence

1. R. G. Collingwood, *The Idea of History*, New York: Oxford University Press, 1956.
2. Erik H. Erikson, "The Dream Specimen of Psychoanalysis," *Journal of the American Psychoanalytic Association*, 2:5–56, 1954.
3. Erik H. Erikson, "Identity and the Lifecycle," Monograph, *Psychological Issues*, Vol. I, No. 1, New York: International Universities Press, 1959.
4. Erik H. Erikson, "Youth: Fidelity and Diversity," *Daedalus*, 91:5–27, 1962.
5. David Rapaport and M. Gill, "The Points of View and Assumptions of Metapsychology," *International Journal of Psycho-analysis*, 40:1–10, 1959.

III Identity and Uprootedness in Our Time

1. David Lerner, *The Passing of Traditional Society*, Glencoe: The Free Press, 1958.
2. See *Uprooting and Resettlement*, Papers presented at the 11th Annual Meeting of the World Federation for Mental Health, Vienna, 1958, Bulletin of the Federation, 1959.
3. *Ibid.*
4. Erik H. Erikson, *Childhood and Society*, Second Edition, New York: W. W. Norton, 1963.
5. See Erik H. Erikson, "Wholeness and Totality," in *Totalitarianism*, Proceedings of a Conference held at the American Academy of Arts and Sciences, edited by C. J. Friedrich, Cambridge: Harvard University Press, 1954.
6. Anna Freud and Sophie Dann, "An Experiment in Group Upbringing," in *The Psychoanalytic Study of the Child*, Vol. VI, New York: International Universities Press, 1951.
7. René Spitz, "Anaclitic Depression," in *The Psychoanalytic Study of the Child*, Vol. II, New York: International Universities Press, 1946.

IV Human Strength and the Cycle of Generations

1. Erik H. Erikson, *Childhood and Society*, Second Edition, New York: W. W. Norton, 1963.
2. Erik H. Erikson, "The Psychosocial Development of Children" and "The Syndrome of Identity Diffusion in Adolescents and Young Adults," in *Discussions in Child Development*, World Health Organization, Vol. III, New York: International Universities Press, 1958.
3. Jean Piaget and B. Inhelder, *The Growth of Logical Thinking from Childhood to Adolescence*, New York: Basic Books, 1958. See also P. H. Wolff, "Piaget's Genetic Psychology and Its Relation to Psychoanalysis," Monograph, *Psychological Issues*, Vol. II, No. 5, New York: International Universities Press, 1960.
4. R. W. White, "Motivation Reconsidered: The Concept of Competence," *Psychological Review*, 66:297-333, 1959.
5. Erik H. Erikson, editor, *Youth: Change and Challenge*, New York: Basic Books, 1963.
6. Erik H. Erikson, "Reflections on Womanhood," *Daedalus*, Spring 1964.
7. Therese Benedek, "Parenthood as a Developmental Phase," *Journal of the American Psychoanalytic Association*, VII, 3, 1959.
8. C. Buehler, *Der menschliche Lebenslauf als psychologisches Problem*, Goettingen: Verlag fuer Psychologie, 1959.
9. Jean Piaget, in *Le Problème des Stades en Psychologie de L'enfant*, Geneva: Presses Universitaires de France, 1955.
10. Erik H. Erikson, *Childhood and Society*, Second Edition, New York: W. W. Norton, 1963.

11. C. H. Waddington, *The Ethical Animal*, London: Allen and Unwin, 1960.
12. Erik H. Erikson, "The Roots of Virtue," in *The Humanist Frame*, edited by Sir Julian Huxley, New York: Harper, 1961.
13. A. Roe and L. Z. Freedman, "Evolution and Human Behavior," in *Behavior and Evolution*, edited by A. Roe and G. C. Simpson, New Haven: Yale University Press, 1958.
14. T. H. Huxley and J. S. Huxley, *Touchstone for Ethics*, New York: Harper, 1947.
15. Sigmund Freud, *The Ego and the Id* [1923], New York: W. W. Norton, 1961.
16. Anna Freud, *The Ego and the Mechanisms of Defense* [1936], New York: International Universities Press, 1946.
17. H. Hartmann, *Ego Psychology and the Problem of Adaptation* [1939], New York: International Universities Press, 1958.
18. *The Letters of William James*, edited by Henry James (his son), Boston: Atlantic Monthly Press, 1920.

V Psychological Reality and Historical Actuality

1. Sigmund Freud, "On the History of the Psycho-analytic Movement" [1904], *Standard Edition*, 14:3–66, London: Hogarth Press, 1957.
2. W. H. Auden, "Greatness Finding Itself," in *Mid-Century*, No. 13, June 1960.
3. H. Hartmann, "On Rational and Irrational Actions," in *Psychoanalysis and the Social Sciences*, Vol. I, New York: International Universities Press, 1947.
4. H. Loewald, "Ego and Reality," *International Journal of Psycho-analysis*, 32:10–18, 1951.
5. H. Hartmann, "Notes of the Reality Principle," in *The Psychoanalytic Study of the Child*, Vol. XI, New York: International Universities Press, 1956.
6. H. Hartmann, *op. cit.* note 3, above.
7. *Ibid.*
8. H. Hartmann, *op. cit.* note 5, above.
9. Sigmund Freud, "A Metapsychological Supplement to the Theory of Dreams" [1917], *Standard Edition*, 14:217–235, London: Hogarth Press, 1957.
10. David Rapaport, "Some Metapsychological Considerations Concerning Activity and Passivity," unpublished manuscript [1953].
11. Sigmund Freud, "Fragment of an Analysis of a Case of Hysteria" [1905], *Standard Edition*, 7:3–122, London: Hogarth Press, 1953.
12. F. Deutsch, "A Footnote to Freud's 'Fragment of an Analysis of a Case of Hysteria,'" *Psychoanalytic Quarterly*, 26:159–167, 1957.
13. Jean Piaget and B. Inhelder, *The Growth of Logical Thinking from Childhood to Adolescence*, New York: Basic Books, 1958.
14. H. Loewald, "On the Therapeutic Action of Psycho-analysis," *International Journal of Psycho-analysis*, 41:16–33, 1960.

15. Sigmund Freud, *The Interpretation of Dreams* [1900], *Standard Edition*, 4, London: Hogarth Press, 1953.
16. *Ibid.*
17. Roy Schafer, "The Loving and Beloved Superego in Freud's Structural Theory," in *The Psychoanalytic Study of the Child*, Vol. XV, New York: International Universities Press, 1960.
18. Bertram Lewin, *Dreams and the Uses of Regression*, New York: International Universities Press, 1958.
19. Sigmund Freud, *The Interpretation of Dreams, op. cit.* note 15, above.
20. Erik H. Erikson, "The Dream Specimen of Psychoanalysis," *Journal of the American Psychoanalytic Association*, 2:5–56, 1954.
21. Erik H. Erikson, *Young Man Luther*, New York: W. W. Norton, 1958.
22. H. Hartmann, *Psychoanalysis and Moral Values*, New York: International Universities Press, 1960.

VI   The Golden Rule in the Light of New Insight

1. C. H. Waddington, *The Ethical Animal*, London: Allen and Unwin, 1960.
2. H. F. Harlow and M. K. Harlow, "A Study of Animal Affection," *The Journal of the American Museum of Natural History*, Vol. 70, No. 10, 1961.
3. Sigmund Freud, *The Origins of Psychoanalysis: Letters to Wilhelm Fliess, Drafts and Notes: 1887–1902*, edited by Marie Bonaparte, Anna Freud and Ernst Kris, New York: Basic Books, 1954.
4. Erik H. Erikson, "Sex Differences in the Play Constructions of Pre-Adolescents," in *Discussions in Child Development*, World Health Organization, Vol. III, New York: International Universities Press, 1958. See also "Reflections on Womanhood," *Daedalus*, Spring 1964.
5. Mahadev Haribhai Desai, *A Righteous Struggle*, Ahmedabad: Navajivan Publishing House, 1951.

Index